W. M. L Jay, A. E Hamilton, L. B Humphrey

He Giveth Songs

A collection of religious lyrics

W. M. L Jay, A. E Hamilton, L. B Humphrey

He Giveth Songs
A collection of religious lyrics

ISBN/EAN: 9783744796323

Printed in Europe, USA, Canada, Australia, Japan

Cover: Foto ©Thomas Meinert / pixelio.de

More available books at **www.hansebooks.com**

HE GIVETH SONGS

A COLLECTION OF RELIGIOUS LYRICS

BY

W. M. L. JAY, A. E. HAMILTON

AND OTHERS

WITH ILLUSTRATIONS BY MISS L. B. HUMPHREY

NEW YORK

E. P. DUTTON AND COMPANY

31 WEST 23D STREET

1885

PREFACE.

IN grief and joy, in shadow and sunshine, by night and day, to men and women of every clime, every age, every degree of poetic talent and culture, " He giveth songs." Their mission of hope, cheer, strength, encouragement, and consolation, is twofold,—first to the special soul that sings, and afterwards to all earnest souls that listen. How well they fulfill this double ministry, may be inferred from the many collections of religious songs that have been made, and, doubtless, will continue to be made. For, as the years go on, there are new songs by new singers; and though the old never cease to delight us with their solidity of thought and the pleasant quaintness of their phraseology and versification, the new wear the kindly charm of every-day likeness—they are the voices of our own time, breathing of our own hopes, fears, needs, and aspirations, and we cannot choose but listen. Yet, wheth-

er the songs be old or new, sung loudly and
clearly, or low and falteringly, by voices trained
and skilled, or careless and untutored, the
burden is always the same,—the great Heart
of Humanity uplifting itself, with more or less
of the patience of hope, to its God ; and waiting—aye, yearning—for the day when it shall
sing the "new song" and drink the "new
wine" of His Kingdom. The voices are many,
but the love and faith are one ; and the con-
cord, we may dare to believe, is sweet not
only to our earthly ears, but to that Divine
Listener who scorns not to receive as our gifts
to Him that which He first so richly bestowed
on us.

This collection is made up of songs old and
new, known and unknown, ancient and mod-
ern,—put side by side, the better to allow of
comparison, and bring out the charm of con-
trast.   It is drawn from many sources,—
former collections, old magazines and news-
papers, in a few cases from tenacious memories ; but, for obvious reasons, poems have
been preferred which are not comprised in
other collections of the day. So far as possible, the names of the authors are given ; two
only are represented so largely as to appear
on the title-page.   One of these is so well

known as the author of "Shiloh" as to need no further introduction; of the other it may not be amiss to speak briefly.

Miss Anna E. Hamilton died early in 1876, at Castle Hamilton, Killeshandra, Ireland, where her short life of about thirty years had been quietly spent. One who knew her well writes enthusiastically of the beauty of her face and character, describes the charming Irish scenery which surrounded her home and fed her imagination, and draws a pleasant picture of her among the tenantry of the estate, ministering to their needs and teaching their children,—literally translating into action what she "taught in song." Her poems first appeared in an English paper called "The Church Bells;" afterwards they were issued in three thin, unpretentious volumes. They were favorably received and reviewed; but they are almost unknown in this country. They are original in style and conception; for the most part short,—strictly confined to one thought, one simile, which is briefly and tersely, often exquisitely, expressed. We are sure that to be loved, they only need to be known.

CONTENTS.

GOD'S PROMISES

As the deep blue of Heaven bright-
    ens into stars,
  So God's great love shines forth
      in promises,
Which, falling softly through our
    prison bars,
  Daze not our eyes, but with their
      soft light bless.
Ladders of light God sets against
    the skies,
Upon whose golden rungs we step
      by step arise,
Until we tread the
      halls of Para-
      dise.

AT THE EVENING-TIME.

WHEN I am sitting alone,
  At closing of day,
Hearing the bare boughs moan
  Over the way,—
Watching the dark clouds flit
  'Twixt the sunset and me,
Till the last effulgent bit
  Vanishes utterly,—
And up from the quiet nooks
  Of my pleasant room,
Over the prints and the books
  Creepeth the gloom ;
Till each pictured friend's dear face,
  And the crimson rose at my side—
All loveliness, color, and grace—
  Sink in the silent tide ;
And I, bereft and alone,
  Am left 'mid the rising waves,
Hearing the bare boughs moan,
  And counting my graves ;—
There comes—like a bell's far chime
  Over the water at night—
The thought that " At evening-time
  It shall be light."

And lo, through a cloud's gray fringe,
   Faintly doth show
The first soft, silvery tinge
   Of a hidden glow ;
And silently, one by one,
   The dusky draperies part,
Till kindly a star looks down
   Into my waiting heart.
And ever the clouds give place,
   And ever the dusk grows pale,
Till from the moon's bright face
   Droppeth the latest veil ;
And over the prints and the books,
   And the crimson rose at my side,
And into the quiet nooks,
   Floweth a silver tide ;
And all that was dark is light,
   And all that was lost is found,—
Touched with a softer light,
   With serener beauty crowned ;—
And the pictured faces light up,
   Sweeter for banishment,
And my soul, as a crystal cup,
   Fills with content.

So, as nearer me, silent and cold,
   Death rolleth its tide.

And treasures are swept from my hold,
    And friends from my side,—
And something of courage and will,
    And something of hope and delight,
Each day 'neath the waters chill
    Sink out of sight,—
And, ever more weary and lone,
    I am left 'mid the waves,
Hearing my lost hopes moan,
    And counting my graves:—
Nay, more,—when that solemn sea,
    Evermore gathering strength,
Solemnly, swiftly o'er me
    Rolleth its waves at length,—
While faces of friends around,
    And the hushed and shadowed room,
With memory, sight, and sound,
    Drift into gloom,—
I think that those waves as they climb,
    Need not my soul affright,
That still, " At the evening-time,
    It shall be light."

Through the swaying, sombre fringe
    Of the curtained clouds, I know
There will steal some faint, soft tinge
    Of a coming glow,—

Some dusky drapings of fear,
  Some shadowy tremors will part,
Some star of heavenly cheer
  Shine into my heart.
And ever the clouds will give place,
  And ever the dusk grow pale,
Till from my Saviour's face
  Droppeth the last, thin veil,—
And faith in seeing is lost,
  And seeing in loving grows dim,
And nothing is counted as cost
  That hath brought me unto Him.
And all that was dark is bright,
  And all that was pain is peace,
As the Day that shall know no night
  Beginneth, and shall not cease :
And long-lost faces light up,
  Dearer for banishment,—
And my soul, as a deep, deep cup,
  Fills with content.

PARADISE.

Once in a dream I saw the flowers
  That bud and bloom in Paradise ;
  More fair they are than waking eyes
Have seen in all this world of ours.

And faint the perfume-bearing rose,
 And faint the lily on its stem,
And faint the perfect violet,
  Compared with them.

I heard the songs of Paradise;
 Each bird sat singing in his place,—
 A tender song so full of grace,
It soared like incense to the skies.
Each bird sat singing to his mate
 A tender song among the trees;
The nightingale herself were cold
  To such as these.

I saw the fourfold River flow,
 And deep it was, with golden sand;
 It flowed between a mossy land,
With murmured music grave and low.
It hath refreshment for all thirst,
 For fainting spirits strength and rest;
Earth holds not such a draught as this
  From east to west.

The Tree of Life stood budding there,
 Abundant with its twelvefold fruits;
 Eternal sap sustains its roots,
Its shadowing branches fill the air.

Its leaves are healing for the world,
　　Its fruits the hungry world can feed,—
Sweeter than honey to the taste,
　　　　And balm indeed.

I saw the Gate called Beautiful,
　　And looked, but scarce could look within;
　　I saw the golden streets begin,
And outskirts of the glassy pool
O harps, O crowns of plenteous stars,
　　O green palm branches many-leaved,—
Eye hath not seen, nor ear hath heard,
　　　　Nor heart conceived !

I hope to see those things again,
　　But not as once in dream of night,—
　　To see them with my very sight,
And touch and handle and attain ;
To have all Heaven beneath my feet,
　　For narrow way that once they trod,—
To have my part with all the saints,
　　　　And with my God.

THE FOOTPRINT.

As once towards Heaven my face was set,
I came unto a place where two ways met;
Cne led to Paradise, and one away,
And fearful of myself lest I should stray,
     I paused that I might know
Which was the way wherein I ought to go.
The first was one my weary eyes to please,
Winding along through pleasant fields of ease
Beneath the shadows of fair branching trees.
" This path of calm and solitude
Surely must lead to heaven," I cried
     In joyous mood;
"Yon rugged one, so rough for weary feet,
The footpath of the world's too busy street,
Lying amid the haunts of human strife,
Can never be the narrow way of life."
But at that moment I thereon espied
A footprint bearing trace of having bled,
And knew it for the Christ's, so bowed my
     head.
     And followed where He led.

CONSECRATION HYMN.

TAKE my life, and let it be
Consecrated, Lord, to Thee.

Take my moments and my days;
Let them flow in ceaseless praise.

Take my hands, and let them move
At the impulse of Thy love.

Take my feet, and let them be
Swift and "beautiful" for Thee.

Take my voice, and let me sing
Always, only, for my King.

Take my lips, and let them be
Filled with messages from Thee.

Take my silver and my gold;
Not a mite would I withhold.

Take my intellect, and use
Every power as Thou shalt choose.

Take my will, and make it Thine ;
It shall be no longer mine.

Take my heart, it *is* Thine own ;
It shall be Thy royal throne.

Take my love ; my Lord, I pour
At Thy feet its treasure-store.

Take myself, and I will be
Ever, only, *all* for Thee.

———

THE ETERNAL NOW.

" For one day in Thy sight is as a thousand years, and a thousand years as one day."

" Now have I won a marvel and a truth ,"
So spake the Soul and trembled,—" dread and
    ruth
Together mixed ; for I did sin of yore ;
But this (so said I oft) was long ago,—
So put it from me far away ; but lo !
With Thee is neither After nor Before,
O Lord, and clear within the noonlight set
Of one illimitable Present, yet

Thou lookest on my fault as it were now.
So will I mourn and humble me ; yet Thou
Art not as man, that oft forgives a wrong
Because he half forgets it, Time being strong
To wear the crimson of guilt's stain away ;—
For Thou, forgiving, dost so in the Day
That shows it clearest,—in the boundless sea
Of Mercy and Atonement, utterly
Casting our pardoned trespasses behind,—
No more remembered, or to come to mind,
Set wide from us as East from West away.
So now this bitter turns to solace kind ;
And I will comfort me that once of old,
A deadly sorrow struck me, and its cold
Runs through me still ; but this was long ago.
My grief is dull through age, and friends out-
    worn,
And wearied comforters, have long forborne
To sit and weep beside me ;—Lord, yet Thou
Dost look upon my pang as it were now ! "

———

TEARS

   Even here,
From His dear children's eyes, God wipes the
   tear ;

And who would mourn a tear should fill his
    eye,
      For God to dry ?
Angels might envy man his tearful eyes
    When God's hand dries.

———

GONE.

WHAT if the heat and the burden,
    Trouble and toil of our day,
Meet with inadequate guerdon ?
    'Tis but a task by the way.
Others will labor and sorrow,
    Struggle with tare and with thorn,
Filling our places to-morrow,—
    We on our way shall be gone ;—
We shall be gone, past toil, past tears,
Into the peace of the endless years.

What if, ere seed of our sowing
    Showeth or leaflet or shoot,
We must pass onward, unknowing
    What shall be blossom or fruit ?
Sunshine and breeze will befriend it,
    Dewdrops of eve and of dawn ;
Hands be outstretched to defend it
    Haply - though we shall be gone,—

We shall be gone, past want, past woe,
Into the joys which the angels know.

What if our labor seems wasted ?
   What if, of all we have sown,
Never ripe fruit we have tasted,
   Never glad harvesting known ?
Others, in brighter to-morrows,
   Lifting glad songs to the morn,
Richly may reap from our furrows--
   Ripened, though we shall be gone,--
We shall be gone, past songs, past sighs,
Into the fulness of Paradise.

Not to ourselves are we living ;
   Not to ourselves do we die ;
Freely receiving as giving,
   Soul after soul marches by,--
Parts of one mighty procession,
   Stretching from Eden's first dawn
On through large curves of progression,
   Till in the Future 'tis gone,--
Gone from earth's ken, past beat, past breath,
Into the life that is miscalled death.

Out of the strain of the Doing
   Into the peace of the Done ;
Out of the thirst of Pursuing
   Into the rapture of Won ;

Out of gray mist into brightness,
   Out of pale dusk into dawn,—
Out of all wrong into rightness,
   We from these fields shall be gone.
" Nay," say the saints, " not *gone*, but *come*,
Into eternity's Harvest-Home !"

———

AT THE BANQUET.

FROTH, or scum, or sparkling wine,
In that brimming cup of thine ?
Take it without word or sign !

Sweet or bitter though it be,
'Tis the portion mixed for thee,
Out of all the company.

Is it sweet ? Ay, life is fair ;
Yet, sip thou the draught with care,—
Sweets may surfeit unaware.

Bitter ? Quaff, and call it good !
Though by thee not understood,
'Tis a tonic for thy blood.

He who drinketh, looking up
For a blessing on his cup,
Doth with God and angels sup.

AFFLICTIONS.

As a ploughed field,
Left desolate and bare
To winter storms and chilly, frosty air,—
Yet only thus made dreary for awhile,
That richer there the harvest grain may smile;
So is the heart whose sod,
Tender and green,
Hath deeply been
Upturned by God,
Its sprouting blades laid low,—
Yet only broken thus by grief's ploughshare,
That in its furrows He might sow
The seed of righteousness, which shall in-
crease
Until it yield the harvest of eternal peace.

PRAYING IN SPIRIT.

" But thou, when thou prayest, enter into thy closet, and when thou hast shut thy door, pray to thy Father which is in secret."—St. Matt. vi. 6.

I NEED not leave the jostling world,
Or wait till daily tasks are o'er,
To fold my palms in secret prayer
Within the close-shut closet door.

There is a viewless, cloistered room,
    As high as heaven, as fair as day,
Where, though my feet may join the throng,
    My soul can enter in and pray.

When I have banished wayward thoughts—
    Of sinful works the fruitful seed,—
When folly wins my ear no more,
    The closet door is shut indeed.

No human step, approaching, breaks
    The blissful silence of the place ;
No shadow steals across the light
    That falls from my Redeemer's face !

And never through those crystal walls
    The clash of life can pierce its way,
Nor ever can a human ear
    Drink in the spirit-words I say.

One hearkening, even, cannot know
    When I have crossed the threshold o'er,
For He, alone, who hears my prayer,
    Has heard the shutting of the door !

PATIENCE.

" BIDE a wee and dinna weary,"
  Patience quaintly was defined
By a little Scottish maiden ;
  And the sweet words in my mind
Ever linger, like the memory
  Of a beautiful refrain,
Making hours of gloom less dreary
  When I breathe them o'er again.

Fretted by the many crosses
  All must bear from day to day,
Troubled by our cares and losses,
  Each of us hath need to say
To our hearts, impatient, crying
  For the ships so long at sea,
While faith faints and hope is dying,—
  " Dinna weary, bide a wee."

Rainy days each life will sadden,
  Gentle shower or tempest wild
Fall upon us,—blessings gladden
  In their turn.   To every child
Gives the Father, or withholdeth,
  Ever wisely, tenderly ;
Thus our hearts for Heaven He mouldeth,—
  " Dinna weary, bide a wee."

Some there are whom glad fruition
   'Neath the skies may never bless,
Some to whose long-urged petition
   Ne'er will come the yearned-for " Yes."
Why ?   God knoweth,—He who lendeth
   Strength to suffer trustingly ;
What He seeth best He sendeth,—
   " Dinna weary, bide a wee."

Hopeful wait a glad " to-morrow,"
   Cast on Jesus every care ;
Not unseen by Him thy sorrow,
   Not unpitied thy despair.
For His people there remaineth
   Rest and peace eternally,
Where the light of joy ne'er waneth,—
   " Dinna weary, bide a wee."

CARE.

As one who through a tree
   Looks unto distant sunlit hills,
     And cannot see
Their beauty through the branching tracery ;

So we,
From this dark world of which we are so fond,
Through the dense branches of the tree of
care,—
Which, although leafless, all our vision fills,—
Can scarce discern the radiance fair
Of the bright world beyond.

———

TRUST.

WHEN darkness gathers round my path,
And all my song-birds cease to sing,
I know it is not sent in wrath,—
'Tis but the shadow of Thy wing !

When dancing sunbeams round me shine,
And Joy and Peacefulness embrace,
I know the radiance is not mine,—
'Tis just the brightness of Thy face !

THE PULLEY.

" The eye is not satisfied with seeing ; nor the ear with hearing."

WHEN God at first made man,
Having a glass of blessing standing by,—
Let us, said He, pour on him all we can;
Let the world's riches, which dispersèd lie,
    Contract into a span.

So strength first made a way;
Then beauty flowed, then wisdom, honor,
    pleasure ;
When almost all was out, God made a stay,
Perceiving that alone, of all His treasure,
    Rest at the bottom lay.

For if I should, said He,
Bestow this jewel also on my creature,
He would adore my gifts instead of Me,
And rest in nature, not the God of nature;—
    So both should losers be.

Yet, let him keep the rest,
But keep them with repining restlessness;
Let him be rich, and weary,—that at least,
If goodness lead him not, yet weariness
    May toss him to My breast.

SUNSET.

WHEN my sun of life, O Christ, is setting,
Blot out my sins as clouds in love forgetting,
Spreading the crimson of Thy cross's dye
Over my fading sky;—
We only through a crimsoned west
May enter into rest.

———

COUPLETS.

GUEST in a ruinous hut, thou loathest to depart :
Were thine a finer house, 'twould prove a bit-
terer smart.

God's dealings still are love—His chastenings
are alone
Love now compelled to take an altered, louder
tone.

When thou hast thanked thy God for every
blessing sent,
What time will then remain for murmurs or
lament ?

Their windows and their doors some close,—
    and murmuring, say,
The light of heaven ne'er sought into my
    house a way.

God often would enrich, but finds not where
    to place
His treasure,—nor in hand nor heart a vacant
    space.

The oyster sickens while the pearl doth sub-
    stance win ;
Thank God for pains that prove a noble
    growth within.

Some are resigned to go,—might we such
    grace attain,
That we should need our resignation to re-
    main.

God's loudest threatenings speak of love and
    tenderest care,
For who, that wished his blow to light, would
    say, Beware ?

When God afflicts thee, think He hews a
    rugged stone,
Which must be shaped, or else aside as use-
    less thrown.

He knew, who healed our wounds, we quickly
    should be fain
Our old hurts to forget—so let the scars re-
    main.   .

Why win we not at once what we in prayer
    require ?
That we may learn great things as greatly to
    desire.

One furnace, many times, the good and bad
    will hold ;
Yet what consumes the chaff will only cleanse
    the gold.

THAT DAY.

THE earth and heaven were rolled up like a
    scroll ;
  Time and space, change and death, had
    passed away ;
Weight, number, measure, each had reached
    its whole ;
  The Day had come, that day.

Multitudes—multitudes—stood up in bliss,
  Made equal to the angels, glorious, fair;
With harps, palms, wedding garments, kiss of
      peace,
  And crowned and haloed hair.

They sang a song, a new song in the height,
  Harping with harps tó Him who is strong
      and true ;
They drank new wine, their eyes saw with
      new light,
  Lo, all things were made new.

As though one pulse stirred all, one rush of
      blood
  Fed all, one breath swept through them
      myriad-voiced;
They struck their harps, cast down their
      crowns, they stood
  And worshipped and rejoiced.

Each face looked one way like a moon new-
      lit,
  Each face looked one way towards its Sun
      of Love;
Drank love, and bathed in love, and mirrored
      it,
  And knew no end thereof.

Glory touched glory on each blessed head,
　Hands locked dear hands never to sunder
　　more ;
These were the new-begotten from the dead
　Whom the great Birthday bore.

Heart answered heart, soul answered soul at
　　rest,
　Double against each other, filled, sufficed ;
All loving, loved of all ; but loving best
　And best beloved of Christ.

BLIND.

I DO not try to see my way,
　Before, behind, or left, or right ;
I cannot tell what dangers gray
　Do haunt my steps, nor at what height
Above the sea my path doth wind—
　　For I am blind.

If by my side a chasm yawns,
　Oft unawares I pass it by ;
I feel no fear though crimson dawns
　With solemn portents fill the sky ;—
Slow, step by step, my way I find,
　　Patient—and blind.

I know not if my goal doth shine
   Misty and faint in distant blue,
Or if these weary feet of mine
   Its border lands are pressing through;
I question, yet no answer find,
      For I am blind.

On smooth and sunny heights, I laugh,
   In thorny thickets, oft I weep;
Of cool, sweet fountains now I quaff,
   And now of bitter springs drink deep,—
Daring to turn from neither kind,
      Since I am blind.

Yet not without a guide I wend
   My unseen way, by day, by night;
Close by my side there walks a Friend,—
   Strong, tender, true,—I trust His sight;
He sees my way, before, behind,
      Though I am blind.

He leads me as He thinketh best,
   And all the checkered way He knows;
Knows when I need to stop and rest,
   And when to flee from lurking foes,—
Which paths are safe, which undermined
      To trip the blind.

Of all my backward way I know
    But little, save that thus far on
My Friend hath led me safe ; and so
    I trust when once the goal is won,
Good cause of thankfulness to find
        That I was blind.

For in that goal's diviner light,
    And from that Friend's revealèd face,
My thirsty eyes will drink in sight,
    And I shall learn what tender grace
Led me through paths with dangers lined,
        Safely—and blind.

———

"HE SHALL SAVE HIS PEOPLE FROM THEIR SINS."

I MET the Saviour in the evening hours ;
The sun was sinking in the quiet west ;
His hands were filled with newly gathered
    flowers,
With which His Father's mansions should be
    dressed.
I looked upon them with a strange sur-
    prise ;—
He read the thoughts my looks alone ex-
    pressed ;—

"Master, are these indeed earth's very best—
Buds nipped and bitten rudely by the frost—
Blossoms with petals tempest-torn and tost?
And surely Thou hast gathered them with
    cost!"
The Saviour spake with mercy in His eyes,—
    "I came to save the lost."
The Son of Man hath healing for His art;
The withering buds men scornfully despise,
God gathers up and freshens on His heart.

—

PRAYER.

WHEN first thy eyes unveil, give thy soul leave
    To do the like; our bodies but forerun
The spirit's duty. True hearts spread and
    heave
    Unto their God, as flowers do to the sun.
Give Him thy first thoughts then; so shalt
    thou keep
Him company all day, and in Him sleep.

THE NORTH WINDOW.

"THEY will not grow." the grave old gardener
    said,
" No flower that blows could bear such cheer-
    less bed ,
Even ferns and rushes would not lift their
    head.

"So let the pleasant window garden go !
For you, no greenery in the time of snow ;—
For those whose world looks North, it must
    be so."

He spoke so surely that I, just in spite,
Went home, and ere closed in November
　　night,
I made my Northern window gay and bright

With reeds and rushes, grasses, swaying
　　ferns,
And many a flower that in the woodland
　　yearns
For brighter sunshine, yet no stray beam
　　spurns.

" We will look North together, you and I;
No matter what they say, we will not die,—"
I whispered them,—" Let us give song for
　　sigh ! "

For both it was much easier said than done ;
Sometimes we nearly lost the new life won ;
Often we cried in pain, " More sun ! more
　　sun ! "

But yet we lived, and as the days grew long,
Our scanty store of sunbeams grew more
　　strong ;
The ferns and rushes pushed an eager throng

Of blades and leaflets to the gladdening rays:
Their growth was one sweet, silent song of
    praise,—
The tiny forest " lived melodious days."

Stooping, I whispered softly, " Bend your ear
For our own secret, ferns and rushes dear;
Our world looked North—but God, He gave
    good cheer."

———

THE CRUSE THAT FAILETH NOT.

" It is more blessed to give than to receive."

Is thy cruse of comfort wasting? rise and
    share it with another,
And, through all the years of famine, it shall
    serve thee and thy brother;
Love Divine will fill thy storehouse, or thy
    handful still renew ;
Scanty fare for one will often make a royal
    feast for two.

For the heart grows rich in giving ; all its
    wealth is living grain ;
Seeds which mildew in the garner, scattered,
    fill with gold the plain.

Is thy burden hard and heavy ?   Do thy steps
    drag wearily ?
Help to bear thy brother's burden ;   God will
    bear both it and thee.

Numb and weary on the mountains, would'st
    thou sleep amidst the snow ?
Chafe that frozen form beside thee, and to-
    gether both shall glow.
Art thou stricken in life's battle ? — many
    wounded round thee moan ;
Lavish on their wounds thy balsams, and that
    balm shall heal thine own.

Is thy heart a well left empty ?   None but God
    its void can fill ;
Nothing but a ceaseless fountain can its cease-
    less longing still :
Is the heart a living power ?   Self-entwined,
    its strength sinks low ;
It can only live in loving ; and by **serving**,
    love will grow.

———

THINE OWN WAY.

TAKE Thine own way with me, dear Lord,
    Thou canst not otherwise than bless ;
I launch me forth upon a sea
    Of boundless love and tenderness.

I could not choose a larger bliss
   Than to be wholly Thine ; and mine
A will whose highest joy is this,
   To ceaselessly unclasp in Thine.

I will not fear Thee, O my God !
   The days to come can only bring
Their perfect sequences of love,
   Thy larger, deeper comforting.

Within the shadow of this love,
   Loss doth transmute itself to gain ;
Faith veils earth's sorrows in its light,
   And straightway lives above her pain.

We are not losers thus ; we share
   The perfect gladness of the Son,—
Not conquered—for, behold, we reign,
   Conquered and Conqueror are one.

Thy wonderful grand will, my God !
   Triumphantly I make it mine ;
And faith shall breathe her glad "Amen "
   To every dear command of Thine.

Beneath the splendor of Thy choice,
   Thy perfect choice for me, I rest ;
Outside it now I dare not live,
   Within it I must needs be blest.

3

Meanwhile, my spirit anchors calm
  In grander regions still than this;
The fair, far-shining latitudes
  Of that yet unexplored bliss.

Then may Thy perfect, glorious will
  Be evermore fulfilled in me,
And make my life an answering chord
  Of glad, responsive harmony.

Oh, it is life indeed to live
  Within this Kingdom strangely sweet!
And yet we fear to enter in,
  And linger with unwilling feet.

We fear this wondrous rule of Thine,
  Because we have not reached Thy heart;
Not venturing our all on Thee,
  We may not know how good Thou art.

WORRIES.

THE little worries which we meet each day
May lie as stumbling-blocks across our way;
Or we may make them stepping-stones to be
    Of grace, O Christ, to Thee.

"THAT LITTLE."

Tobit iv 8.

" WHAT canst thou do ?" said the oak to the
    flower,
    " With thy little, balmy breath,
        And thy tender cheek's soft glow,
And thy life that is but for an hour,—
    What canst thou do, small flower,
        For a world that is dark with woe,
    And bitter with sin and death ?"

"Ah ! well do I know," sighed the bending
    flower,
    " That my life is humble and fleet,
        And I sweeten but little space ;
Yet many the flow'rets in meadow and bower,
    And if each maketh sweet its hour,
        And its little, quiet place.
    Is not the whole world sweet ?"

———

DYING DEATHS DAILY.

INTO a sorrow-darkened soul
A vision full of peace there stole.

An Angel stood beside her way,
As forth she went at dawn of day,

And said, "O weary and oppressed!
Know that at evening thou shalt rest.

" The cross of sin, the crown of thorn,
The weight of anguish thou hast borne,

" And e'en the sins thou hatest, all
From off thy weary soul shall fall,

" To life and love and peace restored
Within the presence of thy Lord."

Then thankfulness and glad surprise
Flowed from the sorrow-laden eyes.

"With hope of rest so near," said she,
" No sorrow more shall dwell with me.

" No weight of care, no shade of gloom,
Can pass the portal of the tomb;

" And light as air I'll urge my way,
Since burdens fall at close of day."

The Angel lingered, and a smile
Dawned o'er his pitying face the while.

"O weak of heart and hope!" he said,
"Deem'st thou all peace is with the dead?

"Or that thy Lord can dwell more near
To saints in bliss than toilers here?

"If but thou diest day by day
To sins that clog thy homeward way,

"Each night shall be a grave of care,
And morn a resurrection fair,

"And daily be thy strength restored
By the dear presence of thy Lord."

———

THE UNSEEN.

WE walk beneath the shelter of God's wings,
While by our pathway Hope, His angel, sings
Of the unseen and everlasting things.

She sings to us of Heaven, the great Home-
    land,
And our eternal house, "not made with
    hand,"
Preparing for us there by Christ's command.

That not as strangers shall we reach its
    shore,
Friendless, an unknown region to explore;
Our Elder Brother hath gone on before.

———

MY PSALM.

I MOURN no more my vanished years:
    Beneath a tender rain,
An April rain of smiles and tears,
    My heart is young again.

The west winds blow, and singing low,
    I hear the glad streams run;
The windows of my soul I throw
    Wide open to the sun.

No longer forward nor behind
    I look in hope or fear;
But, grateful, take the good I find,
    The best of now and here.

I plough no more a desert land,
    To harvest weed and tare;
The manna dropping from God's hand
    Rebukes my painful care.

I break my pilgrim staff,—I lay
   Aside the toiling oar ;
The angel sought so far away
   I welcome at my door.

The airs of spring may never play
   Among the ripening corn,
Nor freshness of the flowers of May
   Blow through the autumn morn ;

Yet shall the blue-eyed gentian look
   Through fringèd lids to heaven,
And the pale aster in the brook
   Shall see its image given ;—

The woods shall wear their robes of praise,
   The south wind softly sigh,
And sweet, calm days in golden haze
   Melt down the amber sky.

Not less shall manly deed and word
   Rebuke an age of wrong ;
The graven flowers that wreathe the sword
   Make not the blade less strong.

But smiting hands shall learn to heal,—
   To build as to destroy ;
Nor less my heart for others feel
   That I the more enjoy.

All as God wills, who wisely heeds
　　To give or to withhold,
And knoweth more of all my needs
　　Than all my prayers have told!

Enough that blessings undeserved
　　Have marked my erring track;—
That wheresoe'er my feet have swerved,
　　His chastenings turned me back;—

That more and more a providence
　　Of love is understood,
Making the springs of time and sense
　　Sweet with eternal good;—

That death seems but a covered way
　　Which opens into light,
Wherein no blinded child can stray
　　Beyond the Father's sight;—

That care and trial seem at last,
　　Through Memory's sunset air,
Like mountain ranges overpast
　　In purple distance fair;—

That all the jarring notes of life
　　Seem blending in a psalm,
And all the angles of its strife
　　Slow rounding into calm.

And so the shadows fall apart,
　And so the west winds play;
And all the windows of my heart
　I open to the day.

———

SAD AND SWEET.

SAD is our youth, for it is ever going,
　Crumbling away beneath our very feet;
Sad is our life, for it is ever flowing
　In current unperceived, because so fleet;
Sad are our hopes, for they were sweet in
　　　sowing,
　But tares self-sown have overtopped the
　　　wheat;
Sad are our joys, for they were sweet in blow-
　　　ing,—
　And still, oh, still, their dying breath is sweet!
And sweet is youth, although it hath bereft us
　Of that which made our childhood sweeter
　　　still;
And sweet is middle life, for it hath left us
　A newer good to cure an older ill;
And sweet are all things, when we learn to
　　　prize them
Not for their sake, but His, who grants them,
　　　or denies them!

THOU KNOWEST BEST.

IT seems such a woful waste
  Of precious talent and time,
To be lying here day after day,
  Just in my life's best prime,—
With such a weight on my breast,
  And such a mist in my brain,
That I little or nothing know
  Save that living is only pain,—
When I might be doing some work,
  Or saying some helpful word,
To hasten Thy Kingdom on—
  But Thou knowest best, O Lord.

There is so much work to be done!—
  So many mouths to be fed,
So many famishing souls
  Crying for living bread,—
So many little ones lost
  In byways crooked and cold,
To be tenderly sought, and led
  Into Thy safe, sweet fold ;—
It seems that no willing hand
  Rejected should be or ignored,
Not even this poor one of mine—
  But Thou knowest best, O Lord.

Worst of it all, there is need
 Of so much labor within !
Such deep-down rootlets of ill
 So subtly spring up into sin !
It would take my very best powers
 To crop them as fast as they shoot,
And give to the seedlings of grace
 Fair room for blossom and fruit ; —
But closer bound with these pains
 Than with any chain or cord,
I count my lost moments drift by—
 But Thou knowest best, O Lord.

Thou knowest best, inasmuch
 As Thou only art wholly wise ;
Present and Future and Past
 Blend into one in Thine eyes ;
That which we miscall waste
 May be only Thy mystical seed,
Flung wide to make Harvest-Home rich,
 And harvesters blessed indeed,—
May be only the wealth of Thy love
 On an ignorant world outpoured,—
Ah, lavish my days as Thou wilt,
 For Thou knowest best, O Lord !

Thy purposes will not fail
 Because of my idleness,—

The stars in their courses fight
  For the cause which Thou dost bless,—
The angels move at Thy word
  Swifter than light of sun,—
And the patient soul works best
  When it prays, " Thy will be done!"
It may be that never again
  I shall march with the plough or the sword;
It may be—No matter.   Amen ;
  For Thou knowest best, O Lord.

THE TWO TWILIGHTS.

THERE are two twilights unto every day—
Twilight of dawn, and twilight of decay.
    And likewise thus we find
Two twilights in the thinking of mankind—
The twilight of a seeking unto light,
The twilight of a doubting unto night.

"OUR LIGHT AFFLICTION."

LORD, dost Thou call this our affliction
    "light ? "
Is all this anguish little in Thy sight ?

"Child! bring thy balance out. Put in one
    scale
All thine afflictions ; give them in full tale ;
All thy bereavements, grievances, and fears ;
Then add the utmost limit of man's years.
Now, put My Cross into the other side,
That which I suffered when I lived and died."

I cannot, Lord ; it is beyond my might ;
And, lo ! my sorrows are gone out of sight.

" Then try another way. Put in the scale
The Glory now unseen, behind the veil ;
The glory given to thine own estate ;
Use that ' exceeding and eternal weight.'
Which kicks the beam ? "
           Ah, Lord, Thy word is right ;
Thus weighed, my sorrow doth indeed seem
    " light."

———

"THE SOLITARY PLACES SHALL BE GLAD."

How will He make us glad ?
How is that promise sweet to be fulfilled,
    So that our sad,
Our aching hearts be stilled ?

Will He a glory shed
O'er the waste places of our lonely days,
That our bowed head
We can in triumph raise?

Or will there gently steal
A subtle peace and stillness o'er our life,—
O'er woe and weal,—
A hushing of all strife ;—

A calm that naught can break,—
A tender trustfulness that can be " glad,"—
That joy can take
Through good days and through bad ;—

A tender twilight-calm ;—
Such as one sees in far-off Northern days,
That seems a psalm
Of perfect, peaceful praise?

ACCEPTED TIMES.

THERE are immortal moments in each life ;
They come and go,—
One scarce may of their presence know,
Yet in them there is struck a chord,
It may be loud, it may be low,

Of peace or strife,
Of love or hate,
Which will vibrate,
Like circles from a pebble's throw
Unto the coming of the Lord.

———

ISAIAH XXVI. 3.

O SWEET and wondrous promise!
  O Peace that passeth thought!
By God's exceeding goodness
  In trustful spirits wrought!
How doth all earthly pleasure,
  How doth all earthly rest,
Sink into less than nothing
  Beside that Heavenly guest!

No clouds of care that gather,
  No waves of sin that toss,
No blasts of desolation,
  No blight, no strife, no loss,
Shall break the mystic circle
  Of that enshrining peace
Which 'round the steadfast spirit
  Doth grow, and doth not cease.

O rare and gracious promise!
 O Peace, of love the sign !
I long to taste thy sweetness,
 I long to call thee mine.
Descend, O Dove of Heaven,
 O birth-pangs, do not cease,
Till in my chastened spirit
 Is born that Perfect Peace !

———

A SUPPLICATION.

O WAY for all that live! heal us by pain and
  loss ;
 Fill all our years with toil, and bless us with
  thy rod.
Thy bonds bring wider freedom ; climbing,
  by the cross,
 Wins that brave height where looms the city
  of our God !

Hallow our wit with prayer : our mastery
  steep in meekness ;
 Pour on our study inspiration's holy light :
Hew out, for Christ's dear Church, a Future
  without weakness,
  Quarried from thine Eternal Beauty, Order,
  Might !

Met, there, mankind's great Brotherhood of
    Souls and Powers,
  Raise thou full praises from its farthest cor-
    ners dim;
Pour down, O Steadfast Sun, thy beams on all
    its powers;
  Roll through its world-wide spaces Faith's
  . majestic hymn.

Come, age of God's own Truth, after man's
    age of fables!
  Seed sown in Eden, yield the nations' heal-
    ing tree!
Ebal and Sinai, Mamre's tents, the Hebrew
    tables,
  All look towards Olivet, and bend to Calvary.

Fold of the tender Shepherd! rise and spread!
  Arch o'er our frailty roofs of everlasting
    strength!
Be all the Body gathered to its living Head!
  Wanderers we faint: O, let us find our Lord
    at length!

4

THE DECEITFUL HEART.

" WOULD'ST thou glance
Into the dark depths of a human heart
One moment ? "   And Christ set me in a
    trance,
Opening my eyes to see,
While at His word the gates flew wide apart.
I entered and essayed to advance,
But quickly I drew back with sudden start,
Chilled with the coldness of its vaults of sin,
    And all I saw within.
      There
Envy, hatred, malice, pride,
Had each their altars ranged on every side,
To Self, the selfsame idol everywhere ;
While through the cobwebbed windows light
    divine
Struggled to shine.
    " Ah, Lord ! " I cried,
" Surely this heart a heathen's heart must be—
One who has never heard of Thee."
With agony I learned that it was mine.
    I fled away,
O'erwhelmed with sorrow and despair,
To breathe a purer air ;

But in its dismal room
The Christ would stay;—
He shrank not even from this whited tomb,
And it became His temple from that day.

———

GROWING.

UNTO him that hath, Thou givest
   Ever " more abundantly."
Lord, I live because Thou livest,
   Therefore give more life to me;
Therefore speed me in the race,
Therefore let me grow in grace.

Deepen all Thy work, O Master,
   Strengthen every downward root;
Only do Thou ripen faster,
   More and more, Thy pleasant fruit.
Purge me, prune me, self abase,
Only let me grow in grace.

Jesus, grace for grace outpouring,
   Show me ever greater things;
Raise me higher, sunward soaring,
   Mounting as on eagle-wings.
By the brightness of Thy face,
Jesus, let me grow in grace.

Let me grow by sun and shower,
  Every moment water me ;
Make me really hour by hour
  More and more conformed to Thee,
That Thy loving eye may trace,
Day by day, my growth in grace.

Let me, then, be always growing,
  Never, never standing still ;
Listening, learning, better knowing
  Thee and Thy most blessed will,—
Till I reach Thy holy place,
Daily let me grow in grace.

———

THE NAME OF JESUS.

ONE Name alone in all this death-struck earth,
One Name alone come down from highest
    Heaven,
Whence healing and salvation we receive,
    To sinful man is given.

Name brought by Gabriel from the heart of
    God,
And laid like flower-seed in the adoring breast
Of her in whom the mystery was wrought,
    And God made manifest.

O Name of Jesus!—of that lowly Babe,
That on the sunny slopes of Nazareth strayed,
Or, calm and silent on the cottage floor,
      With wild flowers played;

Name of the wondrous Child, that in the tem-
      ple stood,
With brow all meekness, and with eye all light,
Who to the blinded teachers of the Law
      Would have given sight;

Name of the Prophet, Healer, Master, Friend,
Death's mighty Vanquisher, and sorrow's Cure,
The Fountain of new innocence for man,
      That ever shall endure;

The secret, the unutterable Name,
From the world's earlier ages hid so long,
Now in time's fulness given at length to be
      The new creation's song;—

O Name of value infinite! and yet
Thou mov'st our spirits with a deeper thrill,
For the dear lips that have Thy music breathed,
      And then grown still.

For Thou the last gift art our lost ones leave,
To be our comfort on our onward way ;
" Love Jesus," " Jesus is our only hope,"
    Adoringly they say.

As shipwrecked sailors grasp an oar, and
    launch
Upon the billows of a midnight sea,
These fearless souls, embracing Jesus, plunge
    Into Eternity ;

Then, safely floated to the Home of peace,
Where the bright plumèd angels throng the
    shore,
Still, still the Name of Jesus those glad hosts
    In anthems pour.

Name that the ransomed souls forever wear,
Gemmed with pure lustre on each perfect
    brow,
Be Thou the radiance of our earthly lives ;
    Transform us even now.

O Name above all names the most beloved !
Fullest of memories, and of untold peace,
Earnest of all unutterable joys !—
    Yet, fond heart, cease ;

For Jesus is the Name of the High God ;
Hushed be thy thoughts, and silently adore !
When thou shalt come to see Him as He is,
    Thou shalt know more.

———

THE WITHERED LEAF.

I WATCHED a withered leaf borne high
    Upon the wild wind's breath ;
Though upward tossed towards the sky,
    It still remained a thing of death.
On wind of feeling highly wrought,
On wind of intellectual thought,
We unto Christ may nigh be brought,
    A moment brief,
And yet our hearts continue dead
    As that careering withered leaf,
On that autumnal evening red.

———

TRANSVERSE AND PARALLEL.

DEAR Lord, my will from Thine doth run
    Too oft a different way ;
I cannot say, " Thy will be done,"
    In every darkened day ;

My heart grows chill
To see Thy will
Turn all earth's gold to gray.

My will is set to gather flowers,
    Thine blights them in my hand;
Mine reaches for life's sunny hours,
    Thine leads through shadow-land;
        And all my days
        Go on in ways
I cannot understand.

Yet more and more this truth doth shine
    From failure and from loss,—
The will that runs transverse to Thine
    Doth thereby make its cross;
        Thine upright will
        Cuts straight and still
Through pride, and dream, and dross.

But if in parallel to Thine
    My will doth meekly run,
All things in heaven and earth are mine,
    My will is crossed by none.
        Thou art in me,
        And I in Thee,—
Thy will—and mine—are done!

DAY BY DAY.

EVERY day has its dawn,
　Its soft and silent eve,
Its noontide hours of bliss or bale ;—
　Why should we grieve ?

Why do we heap huge mounds of years
　Before us and behind,
And scorn the little days that pass
　Like angels on the wind,

Each turning round a small sweet face
　As beautiful as near ?
Because it is so small a face
　We will not see it clear ;

We will not clasp it as it flies,
　And kiss its lips and brow ;
We will not bathe our weary souls
　In its delicious Now.

And so it turns from us, and goes
　Away in sad disdain ;
Though we would give our lives for it,
　It never comes again.

Yet, every day has its dawn,
Its noontide and its eve ; .
Live while we live, giving God thanks—
He will not let us grieve.

———

THE VIOLETS.

As I was gathering violets in the snow,
Methought how often, when the heart is low,
    And Nature grieves,
The buds of simple faith will meekly blow
    'Neath frosted leaves.

———

YOUR MISSION.

IF you cannot on the ocean
    Sail among the swiftest fleet,
Rocking on the highest billows,
    Laughing at the storms you meet,—
You can stand among the sailors
    Anchored yet within the bay,
You can lend a hand to help them
    As they launch their boats away.

If you are too weak to journey
    Up the mountains steep and high,
You can stand within the valley
    While the multitude go by ;

You can chant a happy measure
　As they slowly pass along,—
Though they may forget the singer,
　They may not forget the song.

If you cannot in the conflict
　Prove yourself a soldier true,
If where smoke and fire are thickest
　There's no work for you to do ;
When the battle-field is silent,
　You can go with careful tread,
You can bear away the wounded,
　You can cover up the dead.

Do not then stand idly waiting
　For some greater work to do ;
Fortune is a fickle goddess,
　She will never come to you.
Go and toil in any vineyard,—
　Do not fear to do and dare ;
If you *want* a field of labor,
　You can find it anywhere.

———

THE CROSS.

SINK in, thou blessèd sign !
　Pass all my spirit through,
And sever with thy sacred touch
　The hollow from the true.

Sorrow shall wear thy badge
   As her fair sign of hope ;
No self-indulgent voice may say
   That grief may have full scope.

Sickness shall own thy sway,
   With steadfast, patient eye,—
Thoughtful for others, who must bear
   The weight of sympathy.

Thou shalt restrain my soul
   'Mid the world's tempting gloss ;
Schemes, memories, wishes, all must feel
   The burden of the Cross.

The understanding high
   Shall bow beneath thy might,
Relinquishing its vain attempt
   To gauge the Infinite.

Through my heart's very ground
   Thy ploughshare must be driven ;
Till all are better loved than self,
   And yet less loved than Heaven.

And my impatient will
   Under Thy yoke shall learn
How to be constant to one end,
   Yet yield at every turn.

On vanity and sin
　Stamp thy broad bars of shame ;
High was my birthright, but my life
　Deserves no meed but blame.

Draw thy clear cutting lines
　In scorn above my pride,
And keep me, with meek wounded heart,
　Close to the Crucified.

Oh! can it, must it be,
　That thou wilt rule all thus?
The cross to Jesus was no dream :
　Shall it be so to us?

———

WINGS.

O THAT my soul had wings ! we sighing cry.
　What wings?　The dove's, to hover round
　　　our nest
On sweet love-errands?　Eagle wings, to fly
　To glory's mountain-crest ?

Or angel wings, to speed on tasks of heaven ?
　Ah ! when God's work demands increase of
　　　powers,
The wider range and freer flight is given,
　If such a task be ours ;

But wings to fly away and be at rest
　　He giveth not ; for whither should we go ?
Away from duty, on an endless quest,
　　Across a sea of woe ?

The fretting friction of our daily life,
　　Heart - weariness　with　loving　patience
　　　　borne,
The meek endurance of the inward strife,
　　The painful crown of thorn,

Prepare the heart for God's own dwelling-
　　　　place,
　　Adorn with sacred loveliness His shrine ;
And brighten every inconspicuous grace,
　　For God alone to shine.

———

"COMPLETE IN HIM."

UNSTABLE waves grow firm below Christ's
　　feet,
　　The wilderness doth blossom as the rose ;
These He doth soften with His mercy sweet,
　　Strengthening the weak and feeble will of
　　　　those.
　　　　　In Him we find
The lacking power of every frame of mind,
　　　　In whom " we are complete."

LIFE'S HISTORY.

" Be merciful, O God, unto Thy people "—Deut. xxi. 8.

LIKE flowing streams our years go by,
   Like filmy smoke our days ;
Between the solemn earth and sky
   We run our thoughtless ways.
We dream of joy, we toil for gold,
   We laugh, love, strive, and hate ;
Our faces, 'neath the quiet mould,
   Are heavenward turned — too late.
      Be merciful, O God !

Ere evil we can know from good,
   Or right from wrong undo,
By mother's milk, by father's blood,
   The evil taints us through.
The sins, the passions, of their past
   Our earliest steps control,
And in our weakness bind us fast,
   Body and brain and soul.
      Be merciful, O God !

Thus fettered, forth we go to meet
   A foe on every hand,—
A foe close-veiled in soft deceit,—
   Smiling, and smooth, and bland ;—

A foe that steals our inmost heart
  With warm and kind embrace,
Till soon or late the maskings part,
  And show the mocking face.
        Be merciful, O God!

So easy, too, the downward way!
  So ready to our feet!
So golden-lined with sunbeams gay,
  And promises most sweet!
For evil meets us everywhere,—
  In daily deed and thought,
In church and mart, in hymn and prayer,—
  The good must still be sought.
        Be merciful, O God!

Beside all waters do we sow,
  And little reap but pain;
Our weary souls "an-hungered" go
  Among the blighted grain,—
Our hungry souls are parched with thirst
  Beside the failing springs;
And all the radiant hopes we nursed
  Depart on lessening wings.
        Be merciful, O God!

Yet, slowly, slowly, day by day,
  We something learn from loss;
From some sweet snares we turn away,
  We half-way lift some cross.

Illusions one by one outworn
   Drop from before our eyes ;
And hands by thorns recurrent torn
   We lift up to the skies.
      Be merciful, O God!

So, daily, nature's weeds grow less,
   The plants of grace grow strong ;
Some sweets we wring from bitterness,—
   We cry, "O Lord, how long !"
We lift our eyes up to the hills,
   We clasp the Holy Rood ;
Thy peace like Heavenly dew distils,—
   We *know* that thou art good
      And merciful, O God !

———

THE RANSOM.

CHRIST did not send,
   But came Himself to save ;
The ransom price He did not lend,
   But gave.
Christ died, the shepherd for the sheep ;
   We only fall asleep.

LOVE AND DISCIPLINE.

SINCE in a land not barren still,
Because Thou dost Thy grace distil,
My lot is fall'n, blest be Thy will !

And since these biting frosts but kill
Some tares in me which choke or spill
That seed Thou sow'st, blest be Thy skill !

Blest be Thy dew, and blest Thy frost,
And happy I to be so crost,
And cured by crosses at Thy cost.

The dew doth cheer what is distrest,
The frosts ill weeds nip and molest,
In both Thou work'st unto the best.

Thus while Thy several mercies plot,
And work on me,—now cold, now hot,—
The work goes on, and slacketh not ;

For as Thy hand the weather steers,
So thrive I best 'twixt joys and tears,
And all the year have some green ears.

THE PATH THROUGH THE SNOW.

BARE and sunshiny, bright and bleak,
Rounded cold as a dead maid's cheek,
Folded white as a sinner's shroud,
Or wandering angel's robes of cloud,—
     Well I know, well I know
Over the fields the path through the snow.

Narrow and rough it lies between
Wastes where the wind sweeps, biting keen;
Every step of the slippery road
Marks where some weary foot has trod;
     Who'll go, who'll go
After the rest on the path through the snow?

They who would tread it must walk alone,
Silent and steadfast—one by one.
Dearest to dearest can only say,
" My heart, I'll follow thee all the way,
      As we go, as we go,
Each after each on this path through the
      snow."

It may be under that western haze
Lurks the omen of brighter days ;
That each sentinel tree is quivering
Deep at its core with the sap of spring,
      And while we go, while we go,
Green grass-blades pierce through the glitter-
      ing snow.

It may be the unknown path will tend
Never to any earthly end,
Die with the dying day obscure,
And never lead to a human door ;
      That none know who did go
Patiently once on this path through the snow.

No matter, no matter ! the path shines plain ;
Those pure snow-crystals will deaden pain ;
Above, like stars in the deep blue dark,
Eyes that love us look down and mark ;—
      Let us go, let us go,
Whither Heaven leads in the path through
      the snow.

AS THOU WILT.

IT is so sweet to live
    My little life to-day,
That I would never leave it, if
    I might forever stay !—
    I sometimes say.

I am so weary, Lord,
    I would lie down for aye,
Could I but hear Thee speak the word:
    " Thy sins are washed away ! "—
    I sometimes say.

The better mood that lies
    These moods between midway,
Comes softly, and I lift mine eyes :
    " Lord, as Thou wilt ! " I pray ;
    And would alway.

———

OUR MASTER.

O LORD and Master of us all !
    Whate'er our name or sign,
We own Thy sway, we hear Thy call,
    We test our lives by Thine.

Thou judgest us ; Thy purity
  Doth all our lusts condemn ;
The love that draws us nearer Thee
  Is hot with wrath to them.

Our thoughts lie open to Thy sight ;
  And, naked to Thy glance,
Our secret sins are in the light
  Of Thy pure countenance.

Thy healing pains ; a keen distress
  Thy tender light shines in ;
Thy sweetness is the bitterness,
  Thy grace the pang, of sin.

Yet, weak and blinded though we be,
  Thou dost our service own ;
We bring our varied gifts to Thee,
  And Thou rejectest none.

To Thee our full humanity,—
  Its joys and pains belong ;
The wrong of man to man on Thee
  Inflicts a deeper wrong.

Who hates, hates Thee ; who loves, becomes
  Therein to Thee allied ;
All sweet accords of hearts and homes
  In Thee are multiplied.

Deep strike Thy roots, O heavenly vine,
  Within our earthly sod,—
Most human and yet most divine,
  The flower of man and God!

———

THE LOWEST PLACE.

Not to be first; how hard to learn
  That lifelong lesson of the Past;
Line graven on line and stroke on stroke;
  But, thank God, learned at last!

So now in patience I possess
  My soul year after tedious year,
Content to take the lowest place,
  The place assigned me here.

Yet sometimes, when I feel my strength
  Most weak, and life most burdensome,
I lift mine eyes up to the hills
  From whence my help shall come.

Yea, sometimes still I lift my heart
  To the Archangel's trumpet-burst,
When all deep secrets shall be shown,
  And many last be first.

TIME'S THREEFOLD ASPECT.

SING, O sighing Heart!
Time is marching on!—
O'er the frost and o'er the snow,
O'er the river's ice-bound flow,
　　Time is marching on!
Decking barren boughs with flowers,
Bringing bird-songs to the bowers,
Gold-embroidering the hours,—
　　Time is marching on!

Sigh, O singing Heart!
Time is marching on!
O'er the sunbeam's golden glow,-
O'er the river's rippling flow,
　　Time is marching on!
Buds and promises he breaks,
Green and ripened fruit he takes,
Down the hoary frost he shakes,—
　　Time is marching on!

Sing not, sigh not, Heart!
Time is marching on!
Neither pains nor pleasures stay,
Work while it is called To-Day,—
　　Time is marching on!

Gloom of eve brings gold of dawning,
Night of death shall be life's morning,—
Take the comfort—heed the warning—
Time is marching on!

———

THE STREAM AND THE ROCK.

O STREAM of love!
If thou should'st come upon a rock of hate,
Rippling around it softly move,
And wait
Till by the rains of grace from heaven fed,
Thou shalt thy waves of mercy o'er it spread!

———

MY SHIPS.

ALL my ships are out at sea;
And the harbors empty lie,
Desolate beneath the eye,
While the waves so fresh and free
Toss my ships upon the sea.

And I know not which are lost,
Buried deeply in the sand;
Neither know I which will land
Worn and altered, tempest-toss'd,—
Mine—though dear has been the cost.

Sailing, sailing, year by year,—
  Some whose value was but small
  Now are prized before them all,
Now have grown to be most dear,—
To my heart of hearts most dear.

Some on which I counted most,
  Deeply laden went to sea;
  But they come not back to me,—
So I fear me they are lost,
Stranded on some alien coast.

Could I stretch a saving hand
  To the ones I hold most dear,
  I would keep it back in fear;
I would wait for them to land,
Standing watching on the strand.

For my ships are not all mine;
  One by one they came to me,
  Sailing slowly o'er the sea;
One by one, in rain or shine,
Find I which are His, which mine.

So I know that I must wait
  Humbly still and patiently
  For my ships to come from sea,—
One by one, or soon, or late,
Sailing through the Golden Gate.

ISAIAH LI. 12.

SWEET is the solace of Thy love,
  My Heavenly Friend, to me,
While through the hidden way of faith
  I journey home with Thee,—
Learning by quiet thankfulness
  As a dear child to be.

Though from the shadow of Thy peace
  My feet would often stray,
Thy mercy follows all my steps,
  And will not turn away,
Yea, Thou wilt comfort me at last,
  As none beneath Thee may.

Oft in a dark and lonely place,
  I hush my hastened breath,
To hear the comfortable words
  Thy loving Spirit saith,
And feel my safety in Thy hand
  From every kind of death.

Oh, there is nothing in the world
  To weigh against Thy will;

Even the dark times I dread the most
    Thy covenant fulfil;
And when the pleasant morning dawns,
    I find Thee with me still.

Then in the secret of my soul,
    Though hosts my peace invade,
Though through a waste and weary land
    My lonely way be made,
Thou, even Thou, wilt comfort me—
    I need not be afraid.

Still in the solitary place
    I would awhile abide,
Till with the solace of Thy love
    My heart is satisfied;
And all my hopes of happiness
    Stay calmly at Thy side.

———

"I AM THAT I AM."

"TELL them I AM," Jehovah said
To Moses, while earth shook with dread;
    And, smitten to the heart,
At once, above, beneath, around,
All Nature, without voice or sound,
        Replied,—"O Lord, THOU ART!"

TWO AND ONE.

The Flesh.

O WEARY burden, ever borne
   Through rough and thorny ways!
O hope and faith, wellnigh outworn,
   So late ye turn to praise!
When shall some little touch of joy
   Crown all these toilsome days!

The Spirit.

O foolish heart, see'st thou no sweet
   In bitter things concealed?
The thorns keep in thy wandering feet,
   The burden is thy shield.
And is there not the "glory" yet
   In heaven to be revealed?

The Flesh.

Ah, me! the way is overlong,
   The glory overfar!
In toiling, I forget hope's song,
   In climbing, lose faith's star!
So far removed those future joys!
   So near my sorrows are!

The Spirit.

No joy so far as Christ from woes
　That scorn His healing grace!
No grief so near as Christ to those
　Who humbly seek His face!
No toil too great to win at last
　At His right hand a place!

Both.

So blind we are,—oh, give us sight!
　So weak,—oh, make us strong!
Touch all our dark with heavenly light,
　Our lips with trustful song;—
So shall no labor seem too hard,
　No way—to Thee—too long!

———

SEEING JESUS.

We would see Jesus! we have longed to see
　　Him
　Since first the story of His love was told;
We would that He might sojourn now among
　　us,
　As once He sojourned with the Jews of old.

We would see Jesus! see the infant sleeping,
  As on our mother's knees we, too, have
    slept ;
We would see Jesus! see Him gently weep-
    ing,
  As we, in infancy, ourselves have wept.

We would behold Him, as He wandered
    lowly,—
  No room for Him, too often, in the inn,—
Behold that life, the beautiful, the holy,
  The only sinless in this world of sin.

We would see Jesus! we would have Him
    with us,
  A guest beloved and honored at our board ;
How blessed were our bread if it were broken
  Before the sacred presence of the Lord !

We would see Jesus! we would have Him
    with us,
  Friend of our households and our children
    dear,—
Who still, should Death and Sorrow come
    among us,
  Would hasten to us, and would touch the
    bier.

We would see Jesus ! not alone in sorrow,
  But we would have Him with us in our
    mirth ;
He, at Whose right hand there are joys for-
    ever,
  Doth not disdain to bless the joys of earth.

We would see Jesus ! but the wish is faith-
    less ;
  Thou still art with us, who hast loved us
    well ;
Thy blessed promise, " I am with you always,"
  Is ever faithful, O Immanuel !

——

THE VALLEY OF DEATH.

I HAVE made Thee my choice,
  O Jesus divine ;
And my heart shall rejoice,
  Thy love it is mine,
      Though I walk in the darkness,
      And walk to my death.

My soul, like a fountain,
  Springs upward to Thee :

And I on the mountain
 Of Zion would be.
  But I stand in the valley
  The Valley of Death!

Descend, angels, this hour,
 Through storm-clouds that roll;
As a little white flower
 Come gather my soul;
  Bear it up on your pinions,
  The swift wings of death.

My full heart is yearning,
 A censer of love:
The sunset is burning
 Like incense above;
  'Tis His token, and gladly
  I walk to my death.

———

THE CHILD ON THE JUDGMENT-SEAT.

WHERE hast thou been toiling all day, Sweet-
  heart,
 That thy brow is burdened and sad?
The Master's work may make weary feet,
 But it leaveth the spirit glad.

6

Was thy garden nipped with the midnight
    frost,
  Or scorched with the mid-day glare?
Were thy vines laid low, or thy lilies crushed,
  That thy face is so full of care?

"No pleasant garden-toils were mine!—
  I have sate on the judgment-seat,
Where the Master sits at eve and calls
  The children around His feet."

How camest thou on the judgment-seat,
  Sweet-heart?   Who set thee there?
'Tis a lonely and lofty seat for thee,
  And well might fill thee with care.

"I climbed on the judgment-seat myself,
  I have sate there alone all day,
For it grieved me to see the children round
  Idling their life away.
They wasted the Master's precious seed,
  They wasted the precious hours;
They trained not the vines, nor gathered the
    fruits,
  And they trampled the meek, sweet flowers."

And what hast thou done on the judgment-
    seat,
  Sweet-heart? What did'st thou there?
Would the idlers heed thy childish voice?
  Did the garden mend for thy care?

"Nay, that grieved me more! I called and I
    cried,
  But they left me there forlorn;
My voice was weak, and they heeded not,
  Or they laughed my words to scorn."

Ah, the judgment-seat was not for thee!
  The servants were not thine!
And the Eyes which adjudge the praise and
    blame
  See farther than thine or mine.
The Voice that shall sound there at eve,
    Sweet-heart,
  Will not raise its tones to be heard;
It will hush the earth, and hush the hearts,
  And none will resist its word.

"Should I see the Master's treasures lost,
  The stores that should feed his poor,
And *not* lift my voice, be it weak as it may,
  And not be grievèd and sore?"

Wait till the evening falls, Sweet-heart,
  Wait till the evening falls;.
The Master is near and knoweth all,
  Wait till the Master calls.
But how fared thy garden-plot, Sweet-heart,
  Whilst thou sat'st on the judgment-seat?
Who watered thy roses and trained thy vines,
  And kept them from careless feet?

" Nay, that is the saddest of all to me!
  That is the saddest of all!
My vines are trailing, my roses are parched,
  My lilies droop and fall."

Go back to thy garden-plot, Sweet-heart!
  Go back till the evening falls!
And bind thy lilies, and train thy vines,
  Till for thee the Master calls.
Go make thy garden fair as thou can'st,—
  Thou workest never alone;
Perchance he whose plot is next to thine
  Will see it, and mend his own.

And the next may copy his, Sweet-heart,
  Till all grows fair and sweet;
And, when the Master comes at eve,
  Happy faces His coming will greet.

Then shall thy joy be full, Sweet-heart,
  In the garden so fair to see,
In the Master's words of praise for all,
  In a look of His own for thee!

———

THE SACRIFICE OF THE WILL.

" Thy will be done."

LAID on Thy altar, O our Lord divine,
  Accept my gift this day, for Jesu's sake!
I have no jewels to adorn Thy shrine,
  Nor any world-famed sacrifice to make;
But here I bring within my trembling hand
  This Will of mine—a thing that seemeth
    small;
And Thou alone, O Lord, canst understand
  How, when I yield Thee this, I yield Thee
    all.
Hidden therein, Thy searching gaze can see
  Struggles of passion, visions of delight—
All that I have, or am, or fain would be—
  Deep love, fond hope, and longings infinite.
It hath been wet with tears, and dimmed with
    sighs,
  Clenched in my grasp till beauty hath it
    none;

Now, from Thy footstool where it vanquished
    lies,
  The prayer ascendeth, "May Thy will be
    done."
Take it, O Father, ere my courage fail,
  And merge it so in Thy own will, that e'en
If in some desperate hour my cries prevail,
  And Thou give back my gift, it may have
    been
So changed and purified, so fair have grown,
  So one with Thee, so filled with peace divine,
I may not know or feel it as mine own,—
  But gaining back my will, may find it
    Thine.

———

THE CROSS.

A CHRISTLESS cross no refuge were for me ;
A crossless Christ my Saviour might not be ;
But, O Christ crucified, I rest in Thee !

———

WINCHESTER CATHEDRAL.

WE stood beside the sculptured screen,
  And heard the holy sound
Of music, from the choir within,
  Filling the silence round.

We heard it rise and float and fall,
　Yet could not catch the words,
Which, to the worshippers within,
　Blent with those solemn chords.

But as each psalm drew near its close,
　We knew that they would raise
Unto the Lord Omnipotent,
　Ascriptions of high praise.

Then we, too, joined, and sang aloud,
　" Glory to God most high,
To Father, Son, and Comforter,
　To all eternity ! "

And thoughts arose of those we love,
　Whose footsteps with us trod
Along the path of life awhile,
　Then mounted to their God.

They scaled the golden steps to Heaven,
　And passed the inner gate ;
We in the outer Church remain,
　Nor understand their state.

We know not what new song they sing,
　Save that they sometimes cry,
" Unto the Lamb that once was slain
　Be praise and majesty ! "

And we may join,—though at our prayers
  On earth no more they bend ;
In adoration of the Lamb,
  Our voices still can blend.

O Thou of Whom the family
  In heaven and earth is named,
For whom such joys Thou hast prepared,
  That Thou art not ashamed

To call us " brethren," and to let
  Our souls through anguish learn
To love, as Thou dost, patiently,
  Without the glad return

From voice of answering love,—without
  The help of sense or sight ;—
Sustain us when we faint and fall,
  Till we are purgèd quite

From all alloy of sin and self,—
  Till we are meet to be
Gathered at last with our beloved,
  Thy countenance to see.

"THERE SHALL BE NO NIGHT THERE."

No night of gloom, to drop between our eyes
    And smiling summer skies ?

No slow-paced night of gnawing pain, to
    creep
    Between our eyes and sleep?

No night of woe, to shut all dear delight
    Out from our longing sight?

No night of sin, to grow and never cease
    Betwixt our hearts and peace ?

No night of death, to darken drearily
    Between our souls and Thee ?

Ah, through these nights guide us, sweet
    Lord, we pray,
    Up to that nightless Day !

THE TURNED LESSON.

" I THOUGHT I knew it ! " she said :
 "I thought I had learned it quite ! "
But the gentle teacher shook her head,
 With a grave, yet loving light
In the eyes that fell on the upturned face,
 As she gave the book
With the mark still set in the self-same place.

"I thought I knew it ! " she said ;
 And a heavy tear fell down
As she turned away with bending head ;
 Yet not for reproof or frown,
And not for the lesson to learn again,
 Or the play hour lost ;
It was something else that gave the pain.

She could not have put it in words,
 But her teacher understood,
As God understands the chirp of the birds
 In the depths of an autumn wood ;
And a quiet touch on the reddening cheek
 Was quite enough ;
No need to question, no need to speak.

Then the gentle voice was heard,
"Now I will try you again,"
And the lesson was mastered, every word;
Was it not worth the pain?
Was it not kinder the task to turn,
Than to let it pass
As a lost, lost leaf that she did not learn?

Is it not often so,
That we only learn in part,
And the Master's testing-time may show
That it was not quite "by heart"?
Then He gives, in His wise and patient grace,
The lesson again,
With the mark still set in the self-same place.

Only stay by His side
Till the page is really known;
It may be we failed because we tried
To learn it all alone.
And now that He would not let us lose
One lesson of love
(For He knows the loss), can we refuse?

But oh! how could we dream
That we knew it all so well,
Reading so fluently, as we deem,
What we could not even spell?

But oh ! how could we grieve once more
That patient One,
Who has turned so many a task before !

That waiting One, who now
Is letting us try again ;
Watching us with the patient brow
That bore the wreath of pain ;
Thoroughly teaching what He would teach,
Line upon line,
Thoroughly doing His work in each.

Then let our hearts be still,
Though our task be turned to-day.
Oh ! let Him teach us what He will,
In His most gracious way,
Till, sitting only at Jesus' feet,
As we learn each line,
The hardest is found all clear and sweet.

———

THE LOST COIN.

LORD, Thou dost enter in,
Into this world of sin,
Sweeping it with the besom of Thy love ;

Searching for that last coin
Which Satan did purloin
From God's great treasury above.
Finding it in the dust,
Thou dost remove its rust;
And, with His image re-impressed once more,
That which was God's Thou dost to God re-
store.

———

BEYOND.

NEVER a word is said,
But it trembles in the air,
And the truant voice has sped,
To vibrate everywhere ;
And perhaps far off in eternal years
The echo may ring upon our ears.

Never are kind acts done
To wipe the weeping eyes,
But like flashes of the sun,
They signal to the skies ;
And up above the angels read
How we have helped the sorer need.

Never a day is given,
But it tones the after years,

And it carries up to heaven
　　Its sunshine or its tears;
While the to-morrows stand and wait,
The silent mutes by the outer gate.

There is no end to the sky,
　　And the stars are everywhere,
And time is eternity,
　　And the here is over there;
For the common deeds of the common day
Are ringing bells in the far-away.

———

THE VOICE WITHIN.

A Voice to me calling—calling!
　　And what doth it say through the shine?
"Oh, life is so vain, with its endless refrain
Of 'That which hath been is what cometh
　　　　again,'—
　　Till Death puts the wretched 'In fine!'"

A Voice to me calling—calling!
　　And what doth it say through the gloom?
"Oh, life is so sweet at the Lord's dear feet;
In the light of His smile it is sequence com-
　　　　plete,
　　And a door into glory, the tomb!"

JACOB'S LADDER.

AH! many a time we look, on starlit nights,
　Up to the sky, as Jacob did of old ; ·
Look longing up to the eternal lights,
　To spell their lines of gold.

But never more, as to the Hebrew boy,
　Each on his way the Angels walk abroad,
And never more we hear, with awful joy,
　The audible voice of God.

Yet, to pure eyes the Ladder still is set,
　And Angel visitants still come and go ;
Many bright messengers are moving yet
　From the dark world below.

Thoughts, that are surely Faith's outspreading
　　wings—
　Prayers of the Church, still keeping time
　　and tryst—
Heart-wishes, making bee-like murmurings,
　Their flower the Eucharist—

Spirits elect, through suffering rendered meet
　For those high mansions—from the nursery
　　door

Bright babes that seemed to climb with clay-
    cold feet
    Up to the Golden Floor,—

These are the messengers forever wending
    From earth to Heaven, that faith alone can
    scan;
These are the Angels of our God, ascending
    Upon the Son of Man!

THE WAVE.

THE wave is mighty, but the spray is weak!
And often thus our great and high resolves,
Grand in their forming as an ocean wave,
    Break in the spray of nothing.

I WILL NOT LET THEE GO.

*And the disciples said, Send her away, for she crieth
after us. But He said, Great is thy faith, be it unto thee
even as thou wilt.*

I WILL not let Thee go, Thou Help in time of
    need!
        Heap ill on ill,
        I trust Thee still,

E'en when it seems as Thou would'st slay in-
deed !
Do as Thou wilt with me,
I yet will cling to Thee ;
Hide Thou thy face, yet, Help in time of need,
I will not let Thee go !

I will not let Thee go ; should I forsake my
bliss ?
No, Lord, thou'rt mine,
And I am Thine,
Thee will I hold when all things else I miss.
Though dark and sad the night,
Joy cometh with the light,
O Thou my Sun, should I forsake my bliss?
I will not let Thee go !

I will not let Thee go, my God, my Life, my
Lord !
Not Death can tear
Me from His care,
Who for my sake His soul in death outpoured.
Thou died'st for love of me,
I say in love to Thee,
E'en when my heart shall break, my God, my
Life, my Lord,
I will not let Thee go !

7

THE WHEREFORE.

GOD only smites, that through the wounds of
　woe
The healing balm He gives may inlier flow.

———

THE ASCENSION.

THE crimson petals of the withering day
　Lay scattered on a bank of evening cloud :
Came twinkling forth upon their glittering way
　The bright forerunners of the starry crowd.
The hazy calmness of the eventide
　Fell softly over mountain, stream and hill ;
Time's greatest day, in all its sunny pride,
　Was gathered to its fathers calm and still.
That day to be remembered evermore,
　When the ascending Lord the heavens
　　bowed :
　　　O Risen Crucified !
Straight from Thy Cross unto Thy Throne we
　soar.

THE GOSPEL FOR THE DAY.

" A PLEASANT room !" the lady said,
   Pausing within the artist's door,
And smiling at the pictured walls,
   The sunshine slanting to the floor.

The artist sighed. —" Yet gladly I
   Would miss that sunshine's fluent gold ;
So oft I think I'm painting warm,
   When I am really painting cold !

"My picture seems so full of sun !—
　I think the whole wide summer lives
And breathes within its little space,
　With all the warmth that summer gives ;

" Till, as the day draws to its close,
　And sunbeams fade along the wall,
I find the sun was in the room,
　Not in my lines and tints at all.

" So, though the sunshine be so sweet,
　So passing fair to heart and sight,
I would my studio looked due North,
　That I might read my work aright.

" If in the North-light cool and pure
　The pictured scenes with summer shine,
I know the sun is in the work,
　The warmth and glow are truly mine.

" But in the sunshine's glamour fair,
　The colors show not truthful-wise ;
And for Art's sake, I well can spare
　All sun, all shine, that cheat my eyes."

It was the Gospel for the Day,
　And haply fell in fertile mould ;—
" My heart and life," she mused, " seem warm ;
Now, would the North-light prove them cold ?

" A temper sweet, a smiling face,—
    Hands not much soiled by shame and sin,—
How much is due to sunny ways?
    How much to light and strength within?

" Should Sorrow pierce me through and
        through,
    Should riches flee on sudden wings,
Would heart and smile keep warm and true
    With joy from still untroubled springs?

" Nay,—more ;—while yet the sunshine falls
    Within my life's large room, must I,
For sake of better work, be fain
    To shut that brightness from my sky?—

" To turn my back on pleasure's sun,
    And hours of dainty ease resign,
That so my life with warmer love
    And richer light may inly shine!

" For Art, and not for God ?—Ah, me !
    Why was the sunshine made so bright?
Why are the children of the world
    Wiser than children of the light? "

So from the artist's sunny room,
    Slow down the shadowy stair she goes,
Within herself still questioning.
    " The answer ?"—That God only knows.

JUDGE NOT.

1 Kings, xviii. 22.

WHERE we but see the darkness of the mine,
God sees the diamond shine.

Where we can only clustering leaves behold,
He sees the bud they fold.

Where we can only threatening clouds descry,
He sees the hidden sky.

Dark is the glass through which we see each
other;
We may not judge a brother.

We only see the rude and outer strife;
God knows the inner life.

Where we our voice in condemnation raise,
God may see fit to praise;

And those, from whom, like Pharisees, we
shrink,
With Christ may eat and drink.

WAITING.

Lord of my nights and days !
  Let my desire be,
Not to be rid of earth,
  But nearer Thee.

If I may nearer draw
  Through lengthened grief and pain,
Then, to continue here,
  Must be my gain ;

Till I have strengthened been
  To take a wider grasp
Of that eternal Life,
  I long to clasp ;

Till I am so refined,
  I can the glory bear
Of that excess of joy,
  I thirst to share ;

Till I am meet to gaze
  On uncreated Light,
Transformed, and perfected,
  By that new sight.

Sorrow's long lesson o'er,
　Death's discipline gone through,
Thou wilt unfold to me
　What joy can do.

Glad souls are on the wing,
　From earth to heaven they flee ;
At last Thine hour will come
　To send for me.

Reveal the mighty love
　That binds Thy heart to mine ;
Thy counsels and my will
　Should intertwine.

Lord of my heart and hopes !
　Let my desire be
Not to be rid of earth,
　But one with Thee.

————

MY VESPER SONG.

FILLED with weariness and pain,
　Scarcely strong enough to pray,
In this twilight hour I sit,
　Sit and sing my doubt away.

O'er my broken purposes,
  E'er the coming shadows roll,
Let me build a bridge of song,
  "Jesus, lover of my soul,

" Let me to thy bosom fly ; "
  How the words my thoughts repeat ;
To thy bosom, Lord, I come,
  Though unfit to kiss thy feet.
Once I gathered sheaves for thee,
  Dreaming I could hold them fast,
Now I can but idly sing,
  "Oh, receive my soul at last."

I am weary of my fears,
  Like a child when night comes on ;
In the shadow, Lord, I sing,
  "Leave, oh leave me not alone."
Through the tears I still must shed,
  Through the evil yet to be,
Though I falter while I sing,
  "Still support and comfort me."

" All my trust on thee is stayed ; "
  Does the rhythm of the song
Softly falling on my heart,
  Make its pulses firm and strong ?

Or is this thy perfect peace,
 Now descending while I sing?
That my soul may sleep to-night,
 " 'Neath the shadow of thy wing."

" Thou of life the fountain art,"
 If I slumber on thy breast,
If I sing myself to sleep,
 Sleep and death alike are rest.
Through the shadows overpast,
 Through the shadows yet to be,
Let the ladder of my song
 " Rise to all eternity."

Note by note its silver bars
 May my soul in love ascend,
Till I reach the highest round,
 In thy kingdom without end.
Not impatiently I sing,
 Though I lift my hands and cry,
" Jesus, lover of my soul,
 Let me to thy bosom fly."

IF THOU COULDST KNOW.

I THINK if thou couldst know,
   O soul that will complain,
What lies concealed below
   Our burden and our pain ;
How just our anguish brings
   Nearer those longed-for things
We seek for now in vain,—
I think thou wouldst rejoice, and not complain.

I think if thou couldst see,
   With thy dim mortal sight,
How meanings, dark to thee,
   Are shadows hiding light ;
Truth's efforts crossed and vexed,
   Life's purpose all perplexed,—
If thou couldst see them right,
I think that they would seem all clear, and
   wise, and bright.

And yet thou canst not know,
   And yet thou canst not see ;
Wisdom and sight are slow
   In poor humanity.
If thou couldst *trust*, poor soul,
   In Him who rules the whole,
Thou wouldst find peace and rest :
Wisdom and sight are well, but Trust is best.

DEATH.

DEATH ! since thy darksome mist
Encircled the all-glorious head of Christ,
    Thou now dost shine
    A halo all divine.

———

MY PRAYER.

WHY should my prayings oft
    In narrow channels run ?—
"Give me of this or that,
    Less shadow, more of sun ! "

I know that all my ways
    In ordered sequence go;
I know that Love Divine
    Appoints my bloom and snow;

I know that where I see
    In part, Thou seest the whole,
That time and life and death
    Are in Thy wise control.

How should my blindness then
  To prompt Thy goodness dare?
Henceforth, in good or ill,
  Be this my humble prayer.—

"Grant me to ask from life
  No more than life can give ;
Grant me to lose in death
  Naught but this life I live."

THANKSGIVING.

I.

THANKS be to God ! to whom earth owes
  Sunshine and breeze,
The heath-clad hill, the vale's repose,
  Streamlet and seas,
The snowdrop and the summer rose,
  The many-voicèd trees.

II.

Thanks for the darkness that reveals
  Night's starry dower ;
And for the sable cloud that heals
  Each fevered flower ;
And for the rushing storm that peals
  Our weakness and Thy power.

III.

Thanks for the sweetly-lingering might
   In music's tone ;
For paths of knowledge, whose calm light
   Is all Thine own ;
For thoughts that at the Infinite
   Fold their bright wings alone.

IV.

Yet thanks that silence oft may flow
   In dew-like store ;
Thanks for the mysteries that show
   How small our lore ;
Thanks that we here so little know,
   And trust Thee all the more.

V.

Thanks for the gladness that entwines
   Our path below ;
Each sunrise that incarnadines
   The cold, still snow ;
Thanks for the light of love, that shines
   With brightest earthly glow.

VI.

Thanks for the sickness and the grief
   That none may flee ;

For loved ones standing now around
    The crystal sea ;
And for the weariness of heart
    That only rests in Thee.

VII.

Thanks for Thine own thrice-blessèd Word,
    And Sabbath rest ;
Thanks for the hope of glory stored
    In mansions blest,
And for the Spirit's comfort poured
    Into the trembling breast.

VIII.

Thanks, more than thanks, to Him ascend,
    Who died to win
Our life, and every trophy rend
    From Death and Sin ;
Till, when the thanks of earth shall end,
    The thanks of heaven begin.

JESU DULCIS MEMORIA.

JESU ! the very thought of Thee
    With sweetness fills my breast ;
But sweeter far Thy face to see,
    And in Thy presence rest.

Nor voice can sing, nor heart can frame,
  Nor can the memory find,
A sweeter sound than Thy blest name,
  O Saviour of mankind !

O Hope of every contrite heart,
  O Joy of all the meek,
To those who fall, how kind Thou art !
  How good to those who seek !

But what to those who find ?   Ah, this
  Nor tongue nor pen can show !
The love of Jesus, what it is,
  None but His loved ones know.

Jesus ! our only joy be Thou,
  As Thou our prize wilt be ;
Jesus ! be Thou our glory now,
  And through eternity.

———

THE PERFECT WILL OF GOD.

As from the bow'd-down branches of the trees
Snow in the sunshine melteth by degrees,
      Leaving them free to rise
      Once more towards the skies ;
So, in the brightness of Thy glance divine,
May sin melt swiftly from this soul of mine.

LOVE'S QUESTIONINGS.

STILL on the lips of all we question
  The finger of God's silence lies.
Shall the lost hands in ours be folded ?
  Will the shut eyelids ever rise ?

O friends ! no proof beyond this yearning,
  This outreach of our souls, we need :
God will not mock the hope He giveth ;
  No love He prompts shall vainly plead.

Then let us stretch our hands in darkness,
  And call our loved ones o'er and o'er :
Some time their arms shall close about us,
  And the old voices speak once more.

———

THE TOUCH OF THE UNSEEN.

As feel the flowers the sun in heaven,
  But sky and sunlight never see ;
So feel I Thee, O God, my God,
  Thy dateless noontide hid from me.

8

As touch the buds the blessed rain,
　But rain and rainbow never see ;
So touch I God, in bliss or pain,
　His far, vast rainbow veiled from me.

Orion, moon and sun and bow
　Amaze a sky unseen by me ;
God's wheeling heaven is there, I know,
　Although its arch I cannot see.

In low estate, I, as the flower,
　Have nerves to feel, not eyes to see ;
The subtlest in the conscience is
　Thyself, and that which toucheth Thee.

Forever it may be that I
　More yet shall feel, but shall not see
Above my soul Thy wholeness roll
　Not visibly, but tangibly.

But flaming heart to rain and ray,
　Turn I in meekest loyalty ;
I breathe, and move, and live in Thee,
　And drink the ray I cannot see.

THE HEM OF HIS GARMENT.

O GOD of Calvary and Bethlehem,
Thou who did'st suffer rather than condemn,
Grant me to touch Thy garment's healing hem!

Thou trailest Thy fair robes of seamless light
Through this dark world of misery and night;
Its blackness cannot mar Thy spotless white.

Thou dost not, Master, as we pass Thee by,
Draw in Thy robes lest we should come too
      nigh;
We see no scorn in Thine all-sinless eye.

There is no shrinking even from our touch;
Thy tenderness to us is ever such,
It can endure and suffer much.

———

EASTER THOUGHTS FOR EASTER FLOWERS.

EASTER blossoms, honeyed blossoms, gathered
      here in holy places,
Rich in odor, warm in color, how ye shame us
      by your graces!

If our lives were plucked this morning, for an
 offering on this altar
(How the thought goes through and through
 us, how our tongues 'mid praises falter !)—

Void of fragrance, void of honey, void of lovely
 form and color,
Ah, how pallid they would seem there, in your
 brightness growing duller !—

Ah, how scentless they would lie there, 'mid
 your wealth of perfume-treasure !
Ah, how quickly they would die there, in His
 glance's stern displeasure !

Spare them, Lord, a little longer, by the might
 of Christ's dear graces,
Through Thy sunshine and Thy rainfall to
 grow sweeter in their places,—

Rich with faith's enshrinèd honey, warm with
 love's heart-crimsoned splendor,
Bright with hope's undying verdure, sweet with
 scent of meekness tender :—

So, when Easter cometh newly, filling up the
 year's completeness,
Lives of ours beside the flowers shall not seem
 all void of sweetness !

LIFE'S TAPESTRY.

Too long have I, methought, with tearful eye
  Pored o'er this tangled work of mine, and
    mused
  Above each stitch awry and thread confused;
Now will I think on what in years gone by
I heard of them that weave rare tapestry
  At royal looms ; and how they constant use
  To work on the rough side, and still peruse
The pictured pattern set above them high.
So will I set my copy high above,
  And gaze and gaze till on my spirit grows
Its gracious impress ; till some line of love
  Transferred upon my canvas, faintly glows ;
Nor look too much on warp and woof, provide
He whom I work for sees their fairer side !

"GATHER UP THE FRAGMENTS."

What life art thou living ?
  A life of giving,—   .
Not of mere golden store,
  But more—much more ?

Is it a shelter ?
  Doth it impart
Love, rest, and thankfulness
  Unto one heart ?

Is it a wilderness,
  Harsh and severe,—
Those who pass over it
  Feeling " How drear ? "

Is it a simple life,
  Soft to the touch,—
Not one of many words,
  But of " love much ? "

Or doth base selfishness
  Lurk, as thine aim,
Through all thy usefulness ?
  Tremble with shame !

Is thine a grateful life,
  True in its tone,—
Yielding in thankfulness
  What God hath sown,—

Sounding an echo meek
  (Heard through the strife—
Trembling, indeed, and weak)
  Of the Great Life ?

If so, thy life may be
　　Humble, unknown :
Yet it is leading thee
　　Up to a throne.

———

THIRTY-FOLD.

"SOME sixty,—some an hundred : "—Why
　　Should not such reckoning have been mine?
　　The seed itself was as divine,
The quickening power as strong : yet I
Bear witness to the increase told,—
　　　　"Some, thirty-fold."

And was the fallow-ground prepared
　　By patient mellowing of the clod,
　　And were the precious rains of God,
So often by the furrow shared,
To yield, with sunshine's added gold,
　　　　But thirty-fold?

And yet the tiller watched the growth,
　　And lopped with constant care away
　　The noxious tares that, day by day,
My heart-soil nurtured, nothing loath
Thereby the stinted gain to hold
　　　　To thirty-fold.

The strengthening of the winter frost
  Was not denied, thro' which the root
  Might strike with deeper, downward shoot,
And back and forth the blade was tost ;
Yet what the count when all is told ?
      Just thirty-fold !

The Master's lowest measure !—When
  He walks his field another year,
  To guard and gauge the ripening ear,
Pray Heaven he may not find again,
That mine lifts upward from the mould
      Still thirty-fold !

O Sower of the seed divine,
  Make it " an hundred ! "—Nevermore
  May I be shamed in counting o'er,
Amid the swath, these grains of mine,
To see the harvest handsel hold
      But thirty-fold !

———

THE BEAUTY OF HOLINESS.

I LOVE Thy skies and sunny mists,
  Thy fields, Thy mountains hoar,
Thy wind that bloweth where it lists,—
  Thy will, I love it more.

I love Thy hidden truth to seek
   All round, in sea, on shore,
The arts whereby like God we speak,—
   Thy will to me is more.

I love Thy men and women, Lord,
   The children round Thy door,
Calm thoughts that inward strength afford,—
   Thy will, O Lord, is more.

But when Thy will my life doth hold,
   Thine to the very core,
The world, which that same will did mould,
   I shall love ten times more.

CALVARY.

John, xviii. 32.

YEA, all the paths of earth lead up to thee,
   O Calvary !
The sad, the pleasant,
   The bond and free,
The prince and peasant,
   As equals meet around thy tree.
The past and present
   Merged into one are found
   Upon thy holy ground.

Darkness and light
Are on Christ's left and on His right,
   But we ourselves must place
   In judgment or in grace.
We may in darkness stand,
Or kneel at His right hand.
      Unheeding of His wistful cry,
      We cannot pass Christ by ;
   We must " Hosanna " sing, or " Crucify,"
   Confess Him or deny.

————

EMPTINESS.

" YET, spite of all, some good work thou hast
      wrought
   In moments snatched from pain's persistent
      sway,
   Some fair fruits plucked along thy thorny
      way,
Some pleasant sheaves from scattered grain-
   rows caught.
Not empty-handed quite shalt thou be brought
   Before the King, but worthy gifts to lay
   At His dear feet." " Sweet friends, I tell
      you, Nay.

Not thus before His throne I stand in thought,
But dumbly holding forth these empty hands
  Full in His sight. Think you He will not
    know
    With what long, weary, wasting, bitter
    stress
Of hope deferred, what precious aims and plans
  Successive crossed, what cherished pride
    brought low,
    What pain, what loss, I bought that empti-
    ness ? "

———

THE SECRET OF A HAPPY DAY.

    JUST to let the Father do
      What He will ;
    Just to know that He is true,
      And be still.
    Just to follow hour by hour
      Where He leadeth ;
    Just to draw the moment's power
      As it needeth.—
  Just to trust Him, this is all !
    Then the day will surely be
  Peaceful, whatsoe'er befall,
    Bright and blessèd, calm and free.

Just to let Him speak to thee
  Through His Word,
Watching, that His voice may be
  Clearly heard.
Just to tell Him everything
  As it rises,
And at once to bring to Him
  All surprises.
Just to listen, and to stay
  Where you cannot miss His voice,—
This is all ! and thus to-day
  Communing, you shall rejoice.

Just to ask Him what to do
  All the day,
And to make you quick and true
  To obey.
Just to know the needed grace
  He bestoweth,
Every bar of time and place
  Overfloweth.
Just to take thy orders straight
  From the Master's own command ;—
Blessed day ! when thus we wait
  Always at our Sovereign's hand.

Just to recollect His love—
  Always true,

Always shining from above,
　　Always new.
Just to recognize its light,
　　All-enfolding ;
Just to claim its present might,
　　All-upholding.
Just to know it as thine own,
　　That no power can take away ;—
Is not this enough alone
　　For the gladness of the day ?

Just to trust, and yet to ask
　　Guidance still,—
Take the training or the task,
　　As He will.
Just to take the loss or gain,
　　As He sends it ;
Just to take the joy or pain,
　　As He lends it.
He who formed thee for His praise
　　Will not miss the gracious aim,—
So to-day, and all thy days,
　　Shall be moulded for the same.

Just to leave in His dear hand
　　Little things,—
All we cannot understand,
　　All that stings.

Just to let Him take the care
Sorely pressing,
Finding all we let Him bear
Changed to blessing.
This is all! and yet the way
Marked by Him who loves thee best,—
Secret of a happy day,
Secret of His promised rest.

———

ALL'S WELL.

THE day is ended. Ere I sink to sleep,
My weary spirit seeks repose in Thine ;
Father, forgive my trespasses, and keep
This little life of mine.

With loving kindness curtain Thou my bed,
And cool in rest my burning pilgrim feet ;
Thy pardon be the pillow for my head,
So shall my rest be sweet.

At peace with all the world, dear Lord, and
Thee,
No fears my soul's unwavering faith can
shake ;
All's well whichever side the grave for me
The morning light may break.

THE PAINTING.

SET a painting in a certain light,
  Only a daub seems there ;
But let the artist find the shade aright,
  It showeth fair.
And thus Christ taketh care
    To scan
Our dark and bright,
  As He, He only, can,
Who is the Maker, Son, and Judge, of Man.

———

"A LITTLE WHILE" AND "FOREVER.'

"FOREVER" they are fading,
  Our beautiful, our bright ;
They gladden us " a little while,"
  Then pass away from sight ;
" A little while " we're parted
  From those who love us best ;
Who gain the goal before us,
  And enter into rest.

Our path grows very lonely,
  And still those words beguile
And cheer our footsteps onward,— ·
  'Tis but " a little while,"—

"A little while" earth's sorrows,
   Its burdens and its care ;
Its struggles 'neath the crosses
   Which we of earth must bear.

There's time to do and suffer,
   To work our Master's will,
But not for vain regretting,
   For thoughts or deeds of ill.
Too short to spend in weeping
   O'er broken hopes or flowers,
Or wandering or wasting,
   Is this strange life of ours.

Though when our cares oppress us,
   Earth's "little while" seems long,
If we would win the battle,
   We must be brave and strong;
That so with humble spirit,
   But highest hopes and aim,
The goal so often longed for
   We may perhaps attain ;—

"Forever" and "Forever"
   To dwell among the blest,
Where sorrows never trouble
   The deep, eternal rest ;

Where one by one we gather
Beneath our Father's smile;
And Heaven's sweet "forever"
Drowns earth's sad "little while!"

"REJOICE WITH THEM THAT DO REJOICE, AND WEEP WITH THEM THAT WEEP."

IF thou art blest,
Then let the sunshine of thy gladness rest
On the dark edges of each cloud that lies
Black in thy brother's skies.
If thou art sad,
Still be thou in thy brother's gladness glad.

NIGHT-SONG.

SLOW, stealing steps of moonlight white
Glide noiselessly about my bed;
I wake from slumbers soft and light,
To think for me Thy blood was shed—
Thy loving heart its life-blood shed.

9

In weary paths of human pain,
    Thy patient feet went to and fro,
To make the way for me more plain,
    And in their track sweet blossoms grow—
    Rare, healing balms and blossoms grow,

Sleep from Thine anguished spirit fled,
    That mine in happy peace may rest ;
Thou had'st not where to lay Thy head,
    That I may slumber on Thy breast—
    Softly and safely on Thy breast.

Thy heart was pierced with scoff and sneer,
    Thy lips endured the traitor's kiss,
Thy friends forsook Thy side in fear,
    That I Thy love may never miss—
    Thy love unfailing may not miss.

On Thee Death all his terrors spent,
    And henceforth waits—a friendly shade—
To show me where Thy footsteps went,
    And lead me after unafraid—
    To follow Thee, Lord, not afraid.

And still, upon Thy throne eterne,
    For human woe and sin and need
Thy heart doth with compassion burn,
    Thy nail-scarred hands uplifted plead—
    Thy kingly lips for me do plead.

So while the silent moonbeans weave
  A silver halo round my sleep,
Let no ill dreams my heart aggrieve,—
  I know Thy love my soul will keep—
  Thy mighty love my soul will keep.

———

THE LOVE OF GOD.

LIKE a cradle rocking, rocking,
  Silent, peaceful, to and fro—
Like a mother's sweet looks dropping
  On the little face below—
Hangs the green earth, swinging, turning,
  Jarless, noiseless, safe and slow,-
Falls the light of God's face bending
  Down and watching us below.

And, as feeble babes that suffer,
  Toss and cry, and will not rest,
Are the ones the tender mother
  Holds the closest, loves the best,—
So when we are weak and wretched,
  By our sins weighed down, distressed—
Then it is that God's great patience
  Holds us closest, loves us best.

O great Heart of God ! whose loving
    Cannot hindered be nor crossed;
Will not weary, will not even
    In our death itself be lost—
Love divine ! of such great loving,
    Only mothers know the cost—
Cost of love, which all love passing,
    Gave a Son to save the lost.

"GREAT IS THY FAITH."

FAITH is a grasping of Almighty power ;
The hand of man laid on the arm of God ;—
    The grand and blessed hour
In which the things impossible to me
Become the possible, O Lord, through Thee.

OFFERINGS.

LORD, I had planned to do Thee service true,
To be more humbly watchful unto prayer,
More faithful in obedience to Thy Word,
More bent to put away all earthly care.

I thought of sad hearts comforted and healed,
Of wanderers turned into the pleasant way,
Of little ones preserved from sin and snare,
Of dark homes brightened with a heavenly ray ;

Of time all consecrated to Thy will,
Of strength spent gladly for Thee, day by day,—
When suddenly the mandate came
That I should give it all, at once, away.

Thy blessed Hand came forth, and laid me
    down,
Turned every beating pulse to throbs of pain,
Hushed all my prayers into one feeble cry,
Then bade me to believe that loss was gain.

And *was* it loss to have indulged such hopes ?—
Nay, they were gifts from out the Inner Shrine,—
Garlands that I might hang about Thy Cross,
Gems to surrender at the call Divine.

As chiselled image unresisting lies
In niche by its own Sculptor's hand designed,
So, to my unemployed and silent life,
Let me in quiet meekness be resigned.

Thou art our Pattern, to the end of time,
O Crucified ! and perfect is Thy Will.
The workers follow Thee in doing good ;
The helpless think of Calvary—and are still.

HOPE IN TROUBLE.

WHEN musing Sorrow weeps the past,
　　And mourns the present pain,
'Tis sweet to think of peace at last,
　　And feel that death is gain.

'Tis not that murmuring thoughts arise,
　　And dread a Father's will;
'Tis not that meek submission flies,
　　And would not suffer still ;—

It is that heaven-born Faith surveys
　　The path that leads to light,
And longs her eagle-plumes to raise,
　　And lose herself in sight.

It is that Hope with ardor glows
　　To see Him face to face,
Whose dying love no language knows
　　Sufficient art to trace.

MY FRIEND.

At set of sun,
Through musings dun,
A knock broke on my startled ear,
A voice said, sweet and silvern clear,—
"Open, a Friend is at thy door."

I answered slow,—
"No friends I know,
Nor trust in friendship any more,—
Friends sting and flay,
Friends go their way,
And leave one lonelier than before.
Better to dwell apart,
Keeping an empty heart,
Than see love's smile become hate's
    frown,—
Better a stirless gloom,
Shut in a silent room,
Than ghosts slow-gliding up and down."

Again the sweet voice came,—
"Yet open all the same,
For I have need of thee,
Though thou hast none of me,—

I hunger, thirst, am naked, sick, and poor ;
   The weary sun is set,
   My locks with dews are wet,
My face with tears,—I pray thee, ope thy door."

   Such plea I could not choose
   Unpitying to refuse,
   Yet half-reluctant still the bars I drew,
   Gave food and wine,
   Garments of mine
   Mended and cleansed to look like new,—
   Nay, more, as love with labor grew,
   And patient use brought skill,
   Turned nurse with right good will ;—
   Lastly, my scanty purse did part
   With him who so had won my heart.

   O wondrous change and rare !
   In royal garments drest,
   Not suppliant, but KING, stood there,
   And clasped me to His breast,—
   Not guest, but Host,
   Who, in his turn, fed me at dearest cost,—
   Not pensioner, but Friend—
   A Friend at sorest need,
   Of kindest word and deed,—
   And best of all, a Friend,
Whose love flows on and on, and knows no end.

WINNOWING.

Thou winnowest (marg. reading) *my path and my lying down, and art acquainted with all my ways."*

THOU Searcher of all hearts, look down and
    see,
Not if the chaff doth most abound in me,
But if there be a tithe of grace for Thee.

A tithe for Thee, in all the unfruitful place !
All the day long before the winds of grace
My chaff upriseth in Thy patient face.

My lying-down, my path, my ways, how poor!
My wasted moments' husks bestrew my floor,
Yet still thou searchest by the garner door;

Content to stoop, if so upon the ground
One grain of trust, one ear of love, be found ;
So doth Thy patience, dearest Lord, abound.

Stay, Lord,—the place is very dark,—yet see ;
Bring Thou Thy light, and search the floor for
　　　me ;
Take what Thou findest—all I have for Thee :

Such as it is, Thou wilt not pass it by ;
E'en on my chaff Thou treadest tenderly,—
Is it the wind, or do I hear Thee sigh ?

Ah, loving sigh, that winnowest my floor !
Breathe round my heart's dark chamber ever-
　　　more,
And as Thou winnowest, increase my store.

EMBLEMS OF CHRIST.

I.—THE ROCK.

Thou everlasting Rock!
Our refuge from the overwhelming shock
Of death and hell's surrounding sea;
Steps were hewn out for us in Thee,
That we might climb
Thy height sublime,
And reach God's grand eternity.

2.—THE DOOR.

O Door of Paradise !
Thou art so wide Thou can'st admit us all,
So narrow sin may never through Thee crawl.

3.—THE CORN OF WHEAT.

O Corn of Wheat, which God for us did sow
In the rough furrows of this world of woe,
That thou the Bread of Life for us might be,
To nourish us to all eternity;
Grant us, through faith, O Christ, to feed on
Thee !

4.—THE VINE.

O true and living Viñe,
Bending so low from heaven in Thine endeavor
 To give us all of Thine immortal wine,
  That we may live forever !

5.—THE WAY.

Thou art the Way,
Stretching across earth's shifting sand
 Unto the promised land ;
Walking in Thee our feet can never stray.

6.—THE MORNING STAR.

Thou art the bright and morning star,
  Emmanuel !
Through all the burden of life's day,
  Oh, may my heart's deep well
  Reflect Thy light divine ;
  And in my day's decline,
Rise Thou as Evening Star, and on me shine !

7.—THE LAMB.

Thou art a gentle and most loving Lamb,
  Wounded to give us balm ;
And still, wherever sin doth reign,
  Thou day by day art slain.
When will man cease to give Thee pain ?

8.—THE LION.

Lion of the tribe of Judah,
Thou hast prevailed to break the seals of grace
　For man's lost race.
Guarded by Thee, we fear no more
The lion seeking whom he may devour ;
　He hath no power
　To hurt the sheep
　Whom thou dost keep.
So mighty, yet so gentle, Lord, Thou art,
The lambs may nestle in Thy Lion's Heart !

———

NOT KNOWING.

" Not knowing the things that shall befall me there."—
Acts, xx. 22.

I KNOW not what shall befall me,
　God hangs a mist o'er my eyes,
And so each step of my onward path
　He makes new scenes to rise,
And every joy He sends me, comes
　As a sweet and glad surprise.

I see not a step before me,
　As I tread on another year,

But the past is still in God's keeping,
    The future His mercy shall clear,
And what looks dark in the distance
    May brighten as I draw near.

For perhaps the dreaded future
    Has less bitter than I think ;
The Lord may sweeten the waters
    Before I stoop to drink,
Or, if Marah must be Marah,
    He will stand beside its brink.

It may be He keeps waiting
    Till the coming of my feet,
Some gift of such rare blessedness,
    Some joy so strangely sweet,
That my lips shall only tremble
    With the thanks they cannot speak.

O, restful, blissful ignorance !
    'Tis blessed not to know,
It holds me in those mighty arms
    Which will not let me go,
And hushes my soul to rest
    On the bosom which loves me so.

So I go on not knowing ;
    I would not if I might ;

I would rather walk in the dark with God,
   Than go alone in the light ;
I would rather walk with Him by faith,
   Than walk alone by sight.

My heart shrinks back from trials
   Which the future may disclose,
Yet I never had a sorrow
   But what the dear Lord chose ;
So I send the coming tears back,
   With the whispered word, " He knows."

JUST WHEN THOU WILT.

JUST when Thou wilt, O Master, call !
Or at the noon, or evening fall,
Or in the dark, or in the light,—
Just when Thou wilt, it must be right.

Just when Thou wilt, O Saviour, come,
Take me to dwell in Thy bright home,—
Or when the snows have crowned my head,
Or ere it hath one silver thread.

Just when Thou wilt, O Bridegroom, say,
" Rise up, my love, and come away ! "
Open to me Thy golden gate
Just when Thou wilt, or soon, or late.

Just when Thou wilt,—Thy time is best,—
Thou shalt appoint my hour of rest,
Marked by the Sun of perfect love,
Shining unchangeably above.

Just when Thou wilt !—No choice for me !
Life is a gift to use for Thee ;—
Death is a hushed and glorious tryst
With Thee, my King, my Saviour, Christ !

———

HIS CONDESCENSION.

UNWORTHY, Lord, are we
The latchet of Thy sandals to untie ;
Yet Thou, O God, from Thine eternity
Dost come forth clothed with our humanity ;—
Most wondrous of all wondrous mystery !—
The Maker, and yet Servant, of our race,
Who, in the awful grandeur of Thy grace
Bending before us on Thy human knee,
Dost wash the dust of sin from our poor feet,
That they may tread unchallenged Heaven's
    street !

THE SEA-SIDE WELL.

(There is a spring of sweet water below tide-mark on the coast of Argylshire.)

ONE day I wandered where the salt sea tide
  Backward had drawn its wave,
And found a spring as sweet as ere hill-side
  To wild flowers gave.

Freshly it sparkled in the sun's bright look,
  And 'mid its pebbles strayed,
As if it thought to join a happy brook
  In some green glade.

But soon the heavy sea's resistless swell
  Came rolling in once more,
Spreading its bitter o'er the clear, sweet well,
  And pebbled shore.

Like a fair star thick buried in a cloud,
  Or life in the grave's gloom,
The well, enwrapt in a deep, watery shroud,
  Sank to its tomb.

As one who by the beach roams far and wide,
  Remnants of wreck to save,
Again I wandered where the salt sea tide
  Withdrew its wave ;

10

And there unchanged, no taint in all its sweet,
  No anger in its tone,
Still, as it thought some happy brook to meet,
  The well flowed on.

While waves of bitterness rolled o'er its head,
  Its heart had folded deep
Within itself, and quiet fancies led,
  As in a sleep ;

Till, when the ocean loosed its heavy chain,
  And gave it back to day,
Calmly it turned to its own life again,
  And gentle way.

Happy, I thought, that which can draw its life
  Deep from the nether springs,—
Safe 'neath the pressure, tranquil 'mid the
    strife,
  Of surface things :—

Safe—for the sources of the nether springs
  Up in the far hill lie ;
Calm,—for their life its power and freshness
    brings
  Down from the sky.

So, should temptation threaten, and should sin
   Roll in its whelming flood,
Make strong the fountain of Thy grace within
   My soul, O God !

When sore Thy hand doth press, and waves of
    Thine
   Afflict me like a sea—
Deep calling unto deep,—infuse from Source
    Divine
   Thy peace in me !

And when death's tide, as with a brimful cup
   Over my soul doth pour,
Let hope survive, a well that springeth up
    For evermore !

Above my head, the waves may come and go,
   Long brood the deluge dire,
But life lies hidden in the depths below,
    Till waves retire ;—

Till Death, that reigns with overflowing flood
   At length withdraws its sway,
And life lies sparkling in the light of God
    And endless day.

SACRIFICE.

How doth the law of sacrifice
  Through all Time's checkered reign hold
    good !—
No treasure won till paid the price,
  No loss regained, no ill withstood.

No mortal born without the dew
  Of solemn pain on mother-brow ;
No golden harvest reaped, save through
  The toil and tearing of the plough.

No Job's integrity complete,
  Till tried by fiery touch of woe ;
No widowed, waning years made sweet,
  Till Ruth says, " Bid me not to go ! "

No bloom of rose till long compressed
  In the close bondage of the bud ;
No nation saved, no wrong redressed,
  Without some flow of willing blood.

No world redeemed from shame and sin,
  No Golden Rule of life made plain,
Tlll Pilate's court Christ enters in,
  And on the Mount the Lamb is slain !

Shall we then shrink, when round our brows
  The thorny crown would cut its mark?
When glory of our Father's house
  Must be attained through seas of dark?

No,—bring the thorns!—we bleed and smile,
  And through the gloom we take our way,—
Fixing our patient gaze the while
  On the faint tinge of silver-gray,

That o'er the hills shows tenderly;—
  Till bright the Morning-Star doth rise,
And saith the Saviour,—"Thou, with Me,
  To-day shalt be in Paradise."

———

THE CRUCIFIXION.

ERE yet the early morn did waken,
    Thou, Thou wert taken
    Into the judgment-hall,
    There to be judged for all.
  Guilty of death they found Thee;
In mocking purple and with thorns they
      crowned Thee,—
          Nor did they know,
Thus binding Thee, they did themselves let go.

THE WAITING.

I WAIT and watch : before my eyes,
   Methinks the night grows thin and gray;
I wait and watch the eastern skies,
To see the golden spears uprise
   Beneath the oriflamme of day !

Like one whose limbs are bound in trance,
   I hear the day-sounds swell and grow,
And see across the twilight glance
Troop after troop, in swift advance,
   The shining ones with plumes of snow !

I know the errand of their feet,
   I know what mighty work is theirs ;
I can but lift up hands unmeet
The threshing-floors of God to beat,
   And speed them with unworthy prayers.

I will not dream in vain despair
   The steps of progress wait for me ;
The puny leverage of a hair
The planet's impulse well may spare,
   A drop of dew the tided sea.

The loss, if loss there be, is mine,—
  And yet not mine, if understood ;
For one shall grasp, and one resign,
One drink life's rue, and one its wine,
  And God shall make the balance good.

O power to do ! O baffled will !
  O prayer and action, ye are one !
Who may not strive, may yet fulfill
The harder task of standing still,—
  And good but wished with God is done !

———

HE GIVETH SONGS IN THE NIGHT.

WE praise Thee oft for hours of bliss,
  For days of quiet rest ;
But, oh, how seldom do we feel
  That pain and tears are best !

We praise Thee for the shining sun,
  For kind and gladsome ways ;
When shall we learn, O Lord, to sing
  Through weary nights and days ?

We praise Thee when our path is plain
  And smooth beneath our feet,
But fain would learn to welcome pain,
  And call the bitter sweet.

When rises first the blush of hope,
  Our hearts begin to sing ;
But surely not for this alone
  Should we our gladness bring.

Are there no hours of conflict fierce,
  No weary toils and pains,
No watchings and no bitterness,
  That bring their blessed gains ?—

They bring their blessed gains full well,
  In truer faith and love,
And patience, and sweet gentleness,
  From our dear home above.

Teach Thou our weak and wandering hearts
  Aright to read Thy way,—
That Thou with loving hand dost trace
  Our history every day.

Then every thorny crown of care,
  Worn well in patience now,
Shall grow a glorious diadem
  Upon a faithful brow.

And every word of grief shall change,
  And wave, a blessed flower,
And lift its face beneath our feet,
  To bless us every hour ;

And Sorrow's face shall be unveiled,
  And we at last shall see
Her eyes are eyes of tenderness,
  Her speech but echoes Thee.

THE PILLARS AND THE ROAD.

FAITH and Hope
Are the bright pillars of the Golden Gate,
And on the threshold of the Kingdom wait ;
But Charity, the road, winds onward through
Into the Land where God makes all things new.

AT LAST.

"SHINE on me, Lord, for other light doth
    wane ;
  And love me, Lord, for other love is fled ;
Be Thou my Hope,—all other hope is vain ;
  Be Thou my Joy,—all other joy is dead."

" Dost thou, then, dare to offer these to Me ?—
  The altar cold, whence no more flame leaps
    up,—
The broken crumbs where others feasted free,—
  The dregs remaining in the empty cup !"

" What can I answer Thee ? My lips are dumb,
　Voiceless my shame, and mute my misery ;
Yet if thus empty, broken, cold, I come,
　Is not my need the greater, Lord, of Thee ? "

" I did but try thee.　Know, thy treasures
　　all,—
　Light, love, hope, joy, were My good gifts to
　　thee ;
Which, when they turned to snares, I did re-
　call,
　So thou should'st find them all—and more—
　　in Me."

———

TENDER MERCIES.

TENDER mercies, on my way
　Falling softly like the dew,
Sent me freshly every day,
　I will bless the Lord for you.

Though I have not all I would,
　Though to greater bliss I go,
Every present gift of good
　To Eternal Love I owe.

Source of all that comforts me,
Well of joy for which I long,
Let the song I sing to Thee
Be an everlasting song.

MAXIMUS.

MANY, if God should make them kings,
 Might not disgrace the throne He gave ;
How few who could as well fulfill
 The holier office of a slave !

I hold him great who, for Love's sake,
 Can give with generous, earnest will,—
Yet he who takes, for Love's sweet sake,
 I think I hold more generous still.

I prize the instinct that can turn
 From vain pretence with proud disdain ;
But more I prize a simple heart
 Paying credulity with pain.

It may be hard to gain, and still
 To keep a lowly, steadfast heart ;   .
Yet he who loses has to fill
 A harder and a truer part.

Glorious it is to wear the crown
  Of a deserved and pure success ;
He who knows how to fail has won
  A crown whose lustre is not less.

Great may he be who can command
  And rule with just and tender sway ;
Yet is Diviner wisdom taught
  Better by him who can obey.

Blessed are those who die for God,
  And earn the Martyr's crown of light ;
Yet he who lives for God may be
  A greater Conqueror in His sight.

———

IS IT PEACE ?

2 Kings, ix. 19.

BETTER to be driven
By adverse winds upon the coast of Heaven ;
  Better to be
As it were, shipwrecked upon its rocks
  By fiercest shocks,
Than to sail on across a waveless sea
  Into a Christless immortality.

THE SONG OF THE BRIDE.

CALL all who love Thee, Lord, to Thee ;
 Thou knowest how they long
To leave these broken lays, and aid
 In Heaven's unceasing song ;
How they long, Lord, to go to Thee,
 And hail Thee with their eyes,—
Thee in Thy blessedness, and all
 The nations of the skies.

All who have loved Thee and done well,
 Of every age, creed, clime ;
The host of saved ones from the ends
 And all the worlds of time ;
The wise in matter and in mind,
 The soldier, sage, and priest,
King, prophet, hero, saint, and bard,
 The greatest soul and least ;

The old, and young, and very babe,
 The maiden and the youth,
All re-born Angels of our age,—
 The age of heaven and truth ;
The rich, the poor, the good, the bad,
 Redeemed alike from sin ;—
Lord, close the book of time, and let
 Eternity begin !

GIVING AS THE WORLD GIVES.

OUT on the wayside a little flower pined,
  Soiled with the dust and parched by the heat;
Over the sky came a cloud on the wind,
  Fresh from the ocean's kiss, rosy and fleet,
"Give me one drop," prayed the pale, fainting
    flower,—
  "Only one drop of the dew in thy breast !"
"Nay," said the cloudlet, "I hie to the bower
  Where the rose and the lily are watching
    the west.
One waits for my coming to brighten her
    bloom,
  The other, new sweetness to add to her
    breath."
"With them," cried the flower, "'tis but tint
    and perfume,
  With me, 'tis a matter of life or of death :
They dwell where the sweet-singing brooklet
    goes by,
  And cools the hot air with its moist little feet ;
Thick screen-work of oak leaves above them
    hangs high,
  And shuts out the sun from their virgin re-
    treat ;

But I, on the edge of the dust-powdered way,
  Stand out in the fierce blazing eye of the
     noon ;—
Ah, give but one drop of thy fullness, I pray,
  Lest I should sink in unwakening swoon ! "

But the cloud went its way ; and more fair
     blushed the rose,
  And the lily her daintier odor flung wide,—
Nor came back the cloud at the daylight's still
     close,
  To see where the flow'ret had fallen and died.

CHRIST'S GIVING.

St. John, xv. 13.

THE spirit of self-sacrifice
  Stays not to count its price.
Christ did not of His mere abundance cast
Into the empty treasury of man's store ;
    The First and Last
Gave until even He could give no more :
      His very living,
      Such was Christ's giving.

"TO ABIDE IN THE FLESH IS MORE NEEDFUL."

I WILL take refuge in my God
  From man and sin and woe ;
Fain would I drop this mortal clod,
  To know as angels know,
And love as angels love,
  And be as angels pure ;—
It is all light, pure light above,
  Bliss unalloyed and sure.

But shall I shun the sacred fight
  Which good maintains with ill ?
No ; strong in my Redeemer's might,
  Be mine to wrestle still.
Here only, in this strife,
  Can I His soldier be ;
Here only spend or lose a life
  For Him who died for me.

Nor would I, too impatient, pry
  The awful veil within ;
Or scan th' appalling mystery
  Of God-resisting sin.

Oh, let me be content
For Heaven's own light to stay:
The night—the night is well-nigh spent,—
Ere long it will be day.

———

SAINTS.

THESE " little ones " whom we despise,
These are the saints whom God doth canonize;
Yea, humble names we know not, or forget,
High in the calendar of Heaven are set.
Not lifted eyes,
But contrite hearts, find favor in the skies.

———

SEA-WEED.

NOT always unimpeded can I pray,
Nor, pitying saint, thine intercession claim ;
Too closely clings the burden of the day,
And all the mint and anise that I pay
But swells my debt and deepens my self-blame.

11

Shall I less patience have than thou, who know
That thou revisit'st all who wait for thee,
Nor only fill'st the unsounded deeps below,
But dost refresh with punctual overflow
The rifts where unregarded mosses be ?

The drooping sea-weed hears, in night abyssed,
Far and more far the wave's receding shocks,
Nor doubts, for all the darkness and the mist,
That the pale shepherdess will keep her tryst,
And shoreward lead again her foam-fleeced
      flocks.

For the same wave that rims the Carib shore
With momentary brede of pearl and gold,
Goes hurrying thence to gladden with its roar
Lorn weeds bound fast on rocks of Labrador,
By Love Divine on one sweet errand rolled.

And though Thy healing waters far withdraw,
I, too, can wait and feed on hope of Thee,
And of the dear recurrence of Thy law,—
Sure that the parting grace that morning saw
Abides its time to come in search of me !

IN PORT.

WHEN the great Ship of Life,
Surviving, though shattered, the tumult and
strife
Of earth's angry element,—masts broken short,
Decks drenched, bulwarks beaten,—drives
safe into port ;
When the Pilot of Galilee, seen on the strand,
Stretches over the waters a welcoming hand ;
When, heeding no longer the sea's baffled roar,
The mariner turns to his rest evermore ;
What will then be the answer the helmsman
must give ?
Will it be, " Lo, our log-book ! Thus once we
did live
In the zones of the South ; here, eastward we
turned ;
The stars failed us there ; here, land we dis-
cerned
On our lee ; there, the storm overtook us at
last ;
That day went the bowsprit, the next day the
mast ;
There, the mermen came round us ; and
there, we saw bask
A syren." The Chief of the Port, will He ask

Any one of these questions ?   I cannot think
    so !—
But, " What is the last Bill of Health you can
    show ? "
Not, How fared the soul through the trials
    she passed ?
But, What is the state of that soul at the last ?

———

HIS JEWELS.

In the hush and the gray of the twilight,
    Looking out o'er a shadowy sea,
Half-way between musing and dreaming,
    In a vision it cometh to me,
When the Lord maketh up His jewels,
    What some of my friends will be.

One keeps, in her loving compassion,
    Wide room for all under the sun,
White hands of strong help she outreacheth
    To captive and poor and undone ;—
I know she will shine as a Ruby
    On the breast of the Crucified One.

Another, some wonderful angel,
  In passing, has touched with his wing ;
Her touch has the magic creative,
  Her words can both sparkle and sing ;—
As a Diamond catching the sunlight,
  She will answer the smile of the King.

Still another so richly is dowered
  Through passion and longing and pain,
Through the darkness of deep desolation,
  The pitiless beating of rain ;—
I know I shall see her as Amber
  In the robe of the Lamb that was slain.

As a Priestess of Song, one abideth
  In her place by the altar-side,
And the wine of glad melody poureth,
  The bread of sweet hymns doth divide ;
I think as a Sapphire most precious
  She will deck the pure brow of the Bride.

Deep under her smile, one presseth
  Such pain of bereavement down,—
Such exquisite travail of genius,
  Such rustling of hopes that are brown ;—
As an Opal, far inwardly burning,
  She will shine in the Master's crown.

So still and so holy, one other
　　The darkest of pathways hath trod,
Yet stained no white hem of her garments—
　　Lie softly upon her, O sod !
Meseems as a Pearl that is priceless,
　　She will rest on the bosom of God.

One's soul is an Amethyst tender ;
　　One seemeth an Emerald rare ;
And one in the likeness of Jasper,
　　Of a truth, is surpassingly fair ;—
They will shine as the stars, and forever,
　　In the robe that the Bridegroom doth wear.

O friends, I am glad in your glory,
　　To your preciousness I am made free ;
But why are my longing eyes holden
　　From seeing what cometh to me !
Yet if I with His jewels am numbered,
　　What matters it which I shall be ?

The stars have a differing brightness,
　　Yet all upon each do shine ;
All joy in the wide resplendence,
　　None thinketh of " thine " or " mine " ;—
All know that the source of their glory,
　　O Sun of the Kingdom, is Thine !

THE MYSTERY OF CHASTISEMENT.

" We glory in tribulations."

WITHIN this leaf, to every eye
So little worth, doth hidden lie
Most rare and subtle fragrancy ;

Would'st thou its secret strength unbind ?
Crush it, and thou shalt perfume find,
Sweet as Arabia's spicy wind.

In this dull stone, so poor, and bare
Of shape or lustre, patient care
Will find for thee a jewel rare.

But first must skillful hands essay,
With file and flint, to clear away
The film which hides its fire from day.

This leaf, this stone ! It is thy heart ;
It must be crushed by pain and smart,
It must be cleansed by sorrow's art—

Ere it will yield a fragrance sweet,
Ere it will shine, a jewel meet
To lay before thy dear Lord's feet.

"GOD BE MERCIFUL TO ME, A SINNER!"

WHEN Christ across the tempest of our will
Walketh in grandeur, saying,—" Peace ! be
    still !"
Then shall the surging cares within us cease,
    And we find peace ;—
Yet not a peace self-satisfied, secure,
But earnest, watchful, patient to endure ;—
Not the " I thank Thee " of the Pharisee,
But that of " God be merciful to me !"

———

IN THE GLOAMING.

IN the gloaming, in the gloaming,
    When our thoughts, like bees home-coming,
Stir and buzz about our hearts before they settle
    for the night,
    Come the cares we thought departed,
    Making us once more sore-hearted,
Cares that in the busy sunlight hid themselves
    out of our sight.

For they know the hour is haunted,
That our spirits then are daunted
By the shadows of the darkness that is gather-
  ing o'er our heart ;
And the memories come flocking,
With a stern, resistless knocking,
And our souls, with sorrow filled, at every
  ghostly shadow start.

Can we never quell the aching ?—
Lay the ghosts that thus are taking
From our lives the youth, the freshness, leav-
  ing naught but grief and pain ?
Yes, we know there comes a morrow
Hastened by each God-sent sorrow,
When unanswered human longings will not
  haunt us e'er again.

Then we'll no more dread the gloaming,
Nor the shades of night swift-coming,
For the shadows show the presence of a great,
  if distant, light,
That will break upon our vision,
Shining from the fields Elysian,
Driving ghostly cares and sorrows evermore
  from out our sight.

ANGELS.

" O MESSENGERS of God, are ye beside us ?
　　Fair, loving Angels, are ye tarrying nigh,
With gentle hands for e'er outstretched to
　　　　guide us?"
　　We ask in childhood, looking to the sky.

　　*　　*　　*　　*　　*　　*　　*　　*

A moment's pause !—then, sound through
　　　　silence piercing—
　　Companions shouting from the primrose
　　　　dells --
The thrush his half-learnt roundelay rehears-
　　　　ing—
　　Calls us to earth, and all the dream dispels.

And on through life, longing for hands to guide
　　　　us,
　　Our hearts repeat again with yearning sigh,—
" O messengers of God, are ye beside us ?
　　Strong, loving Angels, are ye tarrying
　　　　nigh ? "

And, asking so, we learn the lesson slowly ;
　　Each day's events may be an Angel sent
With message for the trustful heart and lowly,
　　That holds no idol of self-made intent.

Yea, and the daily things our senses greeting,
  The green bud bursting in the dusky hedge,
The solemn clouds through evening silence
    fleeting,
  Above some city housetop's blackened edge ;

The wandering butterfly, whose pinions flutter
  Adown some narrow street in days of spring,
Have brought sweet thoughts which words
    may never utter,
  Unto the mourning and the suffering.

The fame of lofty deeds, whereat we wonder,
  And hear in them a voice that calls us on ;
The sight of means, whereby good deeds we
    ponder
  Turn by occasion into good deeds done ;

A smile unasked, a wayside salutation,
  The cloudless brightness of some household
    face,—
By these how often God sends forth salvation
  To souls that faint in their appointed place.

Nor always are they messengers whose beauty
  Is to our gaze revealed without disguise ;
They meet us, too, in form of sternest duty,
  Whose guerdon far in the Hereafter lies.

All hours of sorrow, all distress and danger,
  The coming of a thousand daily cares,—
Aye, Death itself may enter as a stranger,
  And prove an Angel honored—unawares.

———

CIRCLES.

As years form circles in the forest tree,
    Each year we see,
Within us, out of sight,
    Maketh a circle for eternity,
Dark or bright.

———

"NO MORE SEA."

" So He bringeth them unto the haven where they would be." Psalms, cvii. 30.

No dash of waters on the rocky shore ?
  No hollow moan in throbbing ocean-caves ?
No hungry breakers' deep and angry roar ?
    No wind-tossed ships ? no wrecks ? no
        watery graves ?
          And no more sea ?
There is the haven, Lord, where we would be !

No surge of sin to beat against the soul ?
  No passion-floods, with legacies of mire ?
No mighty billows of despair to roll
  Unchecked, as sent by God's avenging ire ?
      And no more sea ?
There is the haven where we fain would be !

No chilling tides from icy poles of doubt ?
  No undercurrents of the soul's unrest,
That ever o'er a self-drowned world sends out
  Its winged affections on a fruitless quest ?
      And no more sea ?
'Tis there, O Lord, our weary hearts would be !

No heavy surf of grief, to beat and beat
  Upon the shining sands where Joy doth write
Her rhythmic hopes and promises most sweet,
  And slowly blur and blot them from our
      sight ?
      And no more sea ?
There is the haven where our souls would be ?

Poor, wretched, weak, we shiver on the shore
  Where Death's dread ocean breaketh heav-
      ily ;
Bear us, dear Christ, the misty waters o'er,
  To where that sweet Life-river floweth free—
      But no more sea !
O Blessed Saviour, *there* our souls would be !

"ALL THIS I STEADFASTLY BELIEVE."

YES ! I do feel, my God, that I am Thine !
  Thou art my joy,—myself, my only grief ;
Hear my complaint, low bending at Thy
    shrine,—
    "Lord, I believe ; help Thou mine unbe-
    lief ! "

Unworthy even to approach so near,
  My soul lies trembling like a summer's leaf;
Yet oh, forgive ! I doubt not, though I fear,—
    "Lord, I believe ; help Thou mine unbe-
    lief ! "

True, I am weak, ah, very weak, —but then
  I know the source whence I can draw relief;
And, though repulsed, I still can plead again,
    "Lord, I believe ; help Thou mine unbe-
    lief ! "

Oh, draw me nearer ! far, too far away,
  The beamings of Thy brightness are too
    brief ;
While Faith, though fainting, still hath strength
    to pray,
    "Lord, I believe ; help Thou mine unbe-
    lief ! "

WHO SHALL DELIVER ME ?

GOD strengthen me to bear Myself ;
That heaviest weight of all to bear,
Inalienable weight of care.

All others are outside myself ;
I lock my door and bar them out,
The turmoil, tedium, gad-about.

I lock my door upon myself,
And bar them out ; but who shall wall
Self from myself, most loathed of all ?

If I could once lay down myself,
And start self-purged upon the race
That all must run ! Death runs apace.

God harden me against myself,
This coward with pathetic voice
Who craves for ease and rest and joys :

Myself, arch-traitor to myself ;
My hollowest friend, my deadliest foe,
My clog whatever road I go.

Yet One there is can curb myself,
Can roll the strangling load from me,
Break off the yoke and set me free.

———
.

SYMPATHY.

ASK God to give thee skill
  In comfort's art,
That thou may'st consecrated be
  And set apart
Unto a life of sympathy.
For heavy is the weight of ill
  In every heart ;
And comforters are needed much
  Of Christ-like touch.

———

HYMN OF THE 14TH CENTURY.

FIGHTING the battle of life
  With a weary heart and head,
For in the midst of the strife
  The banners of joy are fled !

Fled and gone out of sight,
　When I thought they were so near, —
And the murmur of hope this night
　Is dying away on mine ear.

Fighting alone to-night—
　With not even a stander-by
To cheer me on in the fight,
　Or to hear me when I cry ;
Only the Lord can hear,
　Only the Lord can see
The struggle within, how dark and drear,
　Though quiet the outside be.

Lord, I would fain lie still
　And quiet, behind my shield ;
But make me to know Thy will,
　For fear I should ever yield.
Even as now my hands,
　So doth my folded will
Lie waiting Thy commands
　Without one anxious thrill.

But as with sudden pain
　My hands unfold and clasp,
So doth my will stand up again
　And taketh its old firm grasp.

12

Nothing but *perfect trust*,
   And love of *Thy perfect will*,
Can raise me out of the dust,
   And bid my fears lie still.

O Lord, Thou hidest Thy face,
   And the battle clouds prevail !
O grant me Thy sweet grace
   That I may not utterly fail !
Fighting alone to-night
   With what a beating heart ;
Lord Jesus, in the fight
   O stand not Thou apart !

HIS GARMENT'S HEM.

THE morning comes across the hills—
   The green and golden hills of June--
And stirs the air with blissful thrills,
   And wakes the landscape into tune.

The lily swings her fragrant bells,
   The birds make vocal all the trees,
And on the beach long tidal swells
   Break into " music of the seas."

The breezes sing their wandering song,
  And every insect's burnished throat
Gives forth its chirp of rapture strong,
  And every wing its strident note.

My lips alone send out no sound,
  No sign of sharing in the strain ;
Yet, Lord, Thou knowest what deep wound
  Is gently closed, and eased of pain.

I seem to touch Thy garment's hem
  In all these wondrous works of Thine ;
And straightway from Thy heart, through them,
  Flows healing virtue into mine.

———

THE KINGDOM OF GOD.

I say to thee—do thou repeat
To the first man thou mayest meet
In lane, highway, or open street,—

That he and we and all men move
Under a canopy of love,
As broad as the blue sky above ;

That doubt and trouble, fear and pain
And anguish, all are shadows vain ;
That death itself shall not remain ;

That weary deserts we may tread,
A dreary labyrinth may thread,
Through dark ways underground be led ;

Yet if one Guide we will obey,
The dreariest path, the darkest way,
Shall issue out in heavenly day ;

And we, on divers shores now cast,
Shall meet, our perilous voyage past,
All in our Father's home at last.

And ere thou leave him, say thou this
Yet one word more,—they only miss
The winning of that final bliss,

Who will not count it true that love,
Blessing, not cursing, rules above,
And that in it we live and move.

And one thing further make him know,—
That to believe these things are so,
This firm faith never to forego,

Despite of all that seems at strife
With blessing, all with curses rife,—
That *this* is blessing, *this* is life.

GRACE FOR GRACE.

GRACE for this day's work or burden,
  Till to-day is yesterday,
And another Grace to-morrow,
  When it shall be called to-day.

Grace, like manna, daily falling ;
  Yet I cannot store away
For to-morrow's need the portion
  Which God gave me yesterday.

As, upon the hallowed table,
  Priestly hands renewed the bread,
So, the old Grace, Christ retaking,
  Grants a fresh supply instead.

One Grace, when sweet revelations
  Pass before my raptured sight,
And my soul is overflowing
  With unspeakable delight,—

And another Grace, sufficient
  For my spirit's direst need,
When some secret thorn is pressing,
  And the path is dark indeed.

Grace in fullness—using rightly,
  To the soul shall more be given,
Interest on interest drawing
  From its treasure laid in heaven.

As the waves in sure succession
  Swell and break upon the shore,
So one Grace breaks o'er another
  On our souls for evermore.

Grace abounding o'er the story
  Of temptation and of sin ;
Grace for Grace, till Grace is Glory
  To the heart that let it in.

DEATH AND THE JEWELS.

" I AM no thief," quoth Death,—" I do but bor-
  row
The treasure that I take from thee to-day ;
Christ will restore thee four-fold on the mor-
  row ;
  For when He comes again, He will repay."

I looked at Death, my heart beat loud and faster:
  " In loan for Christ these treasures I receive;
I am the faithful servant of thy Master ;
  Doubt not," he said, " but earnestly believe."

"Know'st thou," I cried, "that these are all
   my pleasures,
Which thou art bearing to the far-off Land?"
As I reluctantly beheld my treasures
   Shining like pearls in his dim orient hand.

"Fear not," said he, as from my sight he slowly
   Vanished,—the sunlight on his raven wings
Making them shine, half-awful and half-holy,—
   "These are the jewels of the King of Kings.

"These are His jewels, and to Him I bear
   them,
   To deck His robes of immortality;
These are thy treasures, and the Christ will
   wear them,
   That where thy treasures are, thy heart
   may be."

THE VOYAGE OF EARTH.

THIS gray round world, so full of life,
Of hate and love, of calm and strife,
   Still, ship-like, on for ages fares,
And holds its course so smooth and true,—
For all the madness of the crew:—
   It must have better rule than theirs.

QUESTION AND ANSWER.

BEFORE the Sultan's throne appears
　　The Mewlana, with lofty brow.—
" Thy wisdom's fame hath reached mine ears ;
　　Then answer me one question now.

" Four different sects, well knowest thou,
　　My faithful Mussulmans divide ;
And of these four, I fain would know,
　　With which does Allah's favor side ? "

The Sultan spake, and waited dumb :
　　The Mewlana gazed silently
A moment round the audience-room,
　　And then he said, on bended knee ;—

" Thou in whose throne the faithful race
　　The throne of Heaven reflected see ;
Protect me with thy shield of grace,—
　　Then shall my answer be to thee :

" Thou sit'st enthroned here in a hall,
　　To which four doors thy slaves admit,
And all thy splendor bursts on all,
　　Through whichso'er they enter it.

" That I did not mistake the way,
  Thy messenger the praise must claim ;
And, dazzled by the bright display,
  I know not now which way I came."

———

HUMILITY.

HUMILITY befits
The contrite heart that sits
In meek submission at the Saviour's feet ; —
To bend is for the bruisèd reed most meet.

———

THY WAY—NOT MINE.

THY way—not mine, O Lord,
  However dark it be !
Lead me by Thine own hand ;
  Choose out the path for me.

Smooth let it be or rough,
  It will be still the best ;
Winding or straight, it leads
  Right onward to Thy rest.

I dare not choose my lot ;
　I would not, if I might ;
Choose Thou for me, my God,
　So shall I walk aright.

The kingdom that I seek
　Is Thine ; so let the way
That leads to it be Thine,
　Else surely I might stray.

Take Thou my cup, and it
　With joy or sorrow fill ;
As best to Thee may seem,
　Choose Thou my good and ill.

Choose Thou for me my friends,
　My sickness, or my health ;
Choose Thou my cares for me,
　My poverty or wealth.

Not mine—not mine the choice,
　In great things or in small ;
Be Thou my Guide, my Strength,
　My Wisdom, and my All.

THE VINE.

PART I.

A VINE went wandering o'er the ground,
  Half-choked with weeds, oft smeared with
    dust;
  Chance dews it turned to mould and rust,
And nought but leaves was on it found;

Till in its path an Oak-tree stood,
  And round his trunk it skyward twined,
  To learn that oaks were strong and kind,
And feel that higher air was good.

Yet all its bliss it could not know,
  Till—helped by timely suns and showers—
  Its fair new life burst forth in flowers, .
And tiny fruit began to show.

The spheres expanded hour by hour,
   The green through pink to purple grew,
   And, borne on every breeze that blew,
The fragrance sweetened wold and bower.

Yet never boasted once the Vine,—
   " This is my doing ; come and see ! "
   But to the Oak clung gratefully,
And whispered,—" Be the glory thine !

" For had'st thou left me to my will ;
   My devious path, my careless ways,
   My scanty share of dews and rays,
I should be wandering, worthless still."

PART II.

Sun after sun brings vintage-time.
   The Vine is left all brown and bare,—
   Naked—to meet a chiller air,
Empty—to dream of vanished prime.

" Bereaved ! bereaved ! " she moans dis-
      mayed,—
   " My very life-blood slow withdrawn !
   And every day a later dawn,
And every night a longer shade !

" What boots it from that hapless past
   To climb to higher air and worth,
   And gracious bloom and fruit bring forth,
Since to this blank all comes at last ?

" If bliss be open door to pain,
   If most they lose who most possess,
   No more I ask for happiness,—
Give back my ignorance again ! "

" Nay," said the Oak, " not for thine own,
   But others' weal, thou bearest fruit ;
   Thy gain is in thy deeper root,
In twining branches stronger grown,

" And richer store of sap to thrill
   Into new fruitage year by year.
   And though the wintry days be drear,
Does not my strength support thee still ? "

———

A BETTER RESURRECTION.

I HAVE no wit, no words, no tears ;
   My heart within me like a stone
Is numbed too much for hopes or fears ;
   I ook right, look left, I dwell alone ;

I lift mine eyes, but dimmed with grief
  No everlasting hills I see ;
My life is in the falling leaf,—
  O Jesus, quicken me!

My life is like a faded leaf,
  My harvest dwindled to a husk ;
Truly my life is void and brief,
  And tedious in the barren dusk ;
My life is like a frozen thing,
  No bud or greenness I can see ;
Yet rise it shall,—the sap of spring,—
  O Jesus, rise in me !

———

IMPORTUNITY.

HE standeth knocking at the door :—
  "O Lord ! how long ? how long ?
Weeping, Thy patience I adore,
  And yet the bars are strong :
Lord, draw them for me, for my hand is weak,
The night is chill. Enter Thou till the streak
Of ruddy morning flush the day's young
    cheek ! "

He standeth knocking, knocking still ;
   "Sweet, pleading voice, I hear."
The mist is rolling from the hill,
   The fourth slow watch is near :
Through the small lattice I behold His face,
In the cold starlight, full of pitying grace,
Yet—how to guest Him, in so mean a place ?

He standeth knocking, knocking loud !
   Yes ! for the timbers creak :
Eastward there low'rs an angry cloud ;
   "Sweet Saviour, hear me speak ;
Oh, bide not there to feel the drenching rain !
I bid Thee welcome ; but in grief and pain
Tell Thee, my strength against these bars is
   vain."

He standeth knocking, knocking oft,
   The day of grace wears on,
The chiding Spirit whispers soft,
   "Perchance he may be gone
While thou still lingerest." "Not the bars
   alone
Keep Thee out, Lord : against the door is
   thrown
Sand-bags of Care and hoarded gains and
   stone."

He standeth knocking, knocking faint ;
  "Blest Saviour, leave me not ;
But let me tell Thee my complaint,
  The misery of my lot,
And let me sweep the floor Thy feet must
    press,
Deck myself royally for Thy caress,
Make myself worthy, ere Thou stoop to bless ! "

He standeth knocking, knocking still ;
  "Lord, help me in my doubt,
Must I put forth this feeble will
  To draw Thee from without ?
Then help my weakness."   Hear each stern
    bar give,
The door flies backward : He but whispers
    "Live ! "
While on His patient breast I, weeping, plead
    "Forgive ! "

THE FEAST.

" The same spiritual meat, the same spiritual drink."

THOU hast for us a Table spread,
  And we are fed
With costlier than angel's bread,—

Bread from that Corn of Wheat which once
    did die
To yield for man eternally supply,—
        Wine
Pressed from the clusters of the Living Vine;—
This Thou preparest for these guests of Thine,
   And whom dost Thou invite,
   Saying, " Take, eat, and drink ? "
Who may be counted worthy in Thy sight,
   Nor from Thy bidding shrink,—
   The humble or the great ?

" All who do feel their sinfulness and woe,
   Be they of high or mean estate,
   Are welcome, I stoop low.
        Stay !
Wilt thou not also be My guest to-day ? "

HIS SHARE AND MINE.

HE went from me so softly and so soon !—
His sweet hands rest at morning and at noon.

The only task God gave them was to hold
A few fair rosebuds—and be white and cold.

His share of flowers he took with him away ;
No more will blossom here so fair as they.

13

His share of thorns he left,—and if they tear
My hands instead of his, I do not care.

His sweet eyes were so clear and lovely but
To look into the world's wild light—and shut.

Down in the dust they have their share of
    sleep ;
Their share of tears is left for me to weep.

His sweet mouth had its share of kisses,—oh !
What love, what anguish will he ever know ?

Its share of thirst and murmuring and moan
And cries unsatisfied, shall be mine own.

He had his share of summer. Birds and dew
Were here with him,—with him they vanished,
    too.

His share of dying leaves, and rains, and frost,
I take, with every dreary thing he lost.

The phantom of the cloud he did not see
For evermore shall overshadow me.

He, in return, with small, still, snowy feet,
Touched the Dim Path, and made its twilight
    sweet.

THE ELIXIR.

TEACH me, my God and King,
  In all things Thee to see ;
And what I do in anything,
  To do it unto Thee ;

Not rudely, as a beast,
  To run into an action ;
But still to make Thee pre-possest,
  And give it thus perfection.

A man that looks on glass,
  On it may stay his eye ;
Or, if he pleaseth, through it pass,
  And then the heaven espy.

All may of Thee partake ;
  Nothing can be so mean,
Which, with this tincture,—*For Thy sake,*—
  Will not grow bright and clean.

A servant, with this clause,
  Makes drudgery divine ;
Who sweeps a room, as for Thy laws,
  Makes that, and the action, fine.

This is the famous stone
That turneth all to gold ;
For that which God doth touch and own,
Cannot for less be told.

———

INFLUENCE.

THIS learned I from the shadow of a tree,
That to and fro did sway upon a wall,—
Our shadow-selves, our influence, may fall
Where we can never be.

———

THE PHARISAIC WATCH.

*" Why call ye me LORD, LORD, and do not the things which
I say ? "*

" I WAKE, O LORD, and pray,
For night is long and drear."
*" The prayer of night oft needs the light,
To make its meaning clear."*

" I wake, O LORD, and pray,
I tell my sins all o'er."
*" Did'st number first the forest leaves,
The sands along the shore ? "*

"I wake, O LORD, and pray,
 My good deeds, too, I count."
"*Nay, reckon first the pangs I felt
 For thee, on Calvary's mount.*"

"I wake, O LORD, and pray,
 Thy Holy Church defend."
"*For thee I freely gave my life,
 Do thou my vineyard tend.*"

"I wake, O LORD, and pray,
 Help Thou the suffering poor."
"*Nay, did I leave them not with thee?
 They lie before thy door.*"

"I wake, O Lord, and pray,
 My life to Thee I trust."
"*My rain and sunshine bless alike
 The sinful and the just.*"

"I wake, O LORD, and pray,
 Though sore by sleep opprest."
"*Till Conscience wakes, thy watch is vain,
 Sleep on, and take thy rest.*"

"UNTIMELY GATHERED."

" A flower, though offered in the bud,
Is no mean sacrifice."

O FAINTEST Ripple, breaking on the dim
    And utmost shore of life !—
And wert thou all unconscious of the din
    Of outward storm and strife ?
O little Heart, now lying still and cold,
    That beat erewhile with mine, —
O tiny Hands, that lost your feeble hold
    On life, and made no sign !
O little Heart, lying so cold and still,—
    And wilt thou never know
How other hearts thy wavering pulses thrilled
    With their soft ebb and flow ?
How echoes from the future, sweet and far,
    With every stroke kept time ;
And how the tender light of Hope's fair star
    Died one with their low chime ?
O little Soul, while Love and Mystery
    Built thee a fabric bright,
Wert thou not waiting for it patiently
    Beside the gates of light ?
And did'st thou, turning back, grieve sadly o'er
    Thy lost and ruined shrine ?—
And now, oh, wilt thou not for evermore
    Be lost for me and mine ?

Or will the little form unfinished here
  Be perfected for thee,
And still retain in its bright home afar
  Dim memories of me ?
Why are the yearnings of a mother's heart
  So deathless and so strong ?
Why must the life of which thou wast a part
  Cherish the dream so long,
If it be nought beside ?　It cannot be :
  Thus much we know,—
Although we cannot pierce God's mystery,
  He sends not fruitless woe.
Those little sinless feet, undoomed to try
  This rugged world of ours,
Those tender, folded hands, unpiercèd by
  Its thorny flowers,
May lead our thoughts above, and point the
    way ;
  A bliss half-given
May be a link—lest they should turn astray—
  Between our hearts and heaven.
Perhaps we need this bitter drop within
  Life's too alluring cup ;
This our white lamb, a sacrifice for sin,
  Our hearts must offer up.
Who knows but those dumb lips and sealèd
    eyes,
  With eloquence unknown

On earth, may plead for us in Paradise,
  Beside the Golden Throne ?
This folded bud, which, cherished on our
    breast,
  Might gather blight or stain,
In Heaven may bloom more brightly than the
    rest,
  And be our own again.
Howe'er it be, our hearts may not rebel,
  E'en though we grieve,
We know but this,—" He doeth all things
    well."
  We trust and we believe.

———

SUSPIRIA.

TAKE them, O Death ! and bear away
  Whatever thou canst call thine own !
Thine image, stamped upon this clay,
  Doth give thee that,—but that alone !

Take them, O Death, and let them lie
  Folded upon thy narrow shelves,
As garments by the soul laid by,
  And precious only to ourselves !

Take them, O great Eternity !
Our little life is but a gust
That bends the branches of thy tree,
And trails its blossoms in the dust !

———

DARK AND LIGHT.

WHERE the cliff o'erlooks the sea,
I am wondering drearily
Why my life so dark should be ;

While the seas and sands and skies,
Steeped in gorgeous sunset dyes,
With such brightness mock my eyes.

And the sea-gull shows so white,
Far below me skimming light
O'er the crested billows bright,—

Shows so white, my eyes are won
Listlessly to follow on,
Till,—his seaward errand done,—

Swift he takes his upward flight,
Soon to grow as black as night
'Twixt me and the higher light.

Learn, my soul, the lesson due;
Dark and light have much to do
With the gazer's point of view.

If between thy God and thee
Earthly cares float wilderingly,
Dark as night they well may be.

Who would see their wings of white,
Needs must look from Faith's calm height
Downward with undazzled sight.

———

WHAT?

LORD, if Thy wounds have filled the world
 with peace,
What shall Thy joy do, when all sin shall
 cease,
And the new earth shall yield her full increase!

COMMISSIONED.

" Do their errands ; enter into the sacrifice with them ;
be a link yourself in the divine chain, and feel the joy and
life of it."

WHAT can I do for thee, beloved,
Whose feet so little while ago
Trod the same wayside dust with mine,
And now up paths I do not know
Speed, without sound or sign ?

What can I do ? The perfect life
All fresh and fair and beautiful
Has opened its wide arms to thee ;
Thy cup is over-brimmed and full ;
Nothing remains for me.

I used to do so many things
Love thee and chide thee and caress,
Brush little straws from off thy way,
Tempering with my poor tenderness
The heat of thy short day.

Not much, but very sweet to give ;
And it is grief of griefs to bear,
That all these ministries are o'er,
And thou, so happy, love, elsewhere,
Dost need me never more.

And I can do for thee but th's :
(Working on blindly, knowing not
If I may give thee pleasure so ;)
Out of my own dull, shadowed lot
I can arise, and go

To sadder lives and darker homes,
A messenger, dear heart, from thee
Who wast on earth a comforter ;
And say to those who welcome me,
I am sent forth by *her :*

Feeling the while how good it is
To do thy errands thus, and think
It may be, in the blue, far space,
Thou watchest from the heaven's brink,
A smile upon thy face.

And when the day's work ends with day,
And star-eyed evening, stealing in,
Waves her cool hand to flying noon,
And restless, surging thoughts begin,
Like sad bells out of tune,

I'll pray, " Dear Lord, to whose great love
Nor bound nor limit-line is set,
Give to my darling, I implore,
Some new, sweet joy, not tasted yet,
For I can give no more."

And, with the words my thoughts shall climb
  With following feet the heavenly stair
  Up which thy steps so lately sped,
And seeing thee so happy there,
  Come back half comforted.

———

THE SHADED LIGHT.

*"I have yet many things to say unto you, but ye cannot
bear them now."*

As one who entereth by night a room
  Where sufferers lie,
Shadeth his lamp to suit the languid eye ;
  So doth the Christ draw nigh
  Unto our world of gloom.
The light of life He beareth, and doth stand
Shading it tenderly with piercèd hand,
  Lest the full glare
  Should cause us not to see, but stare.
Yet through the nail-prints some sweet rays
  divine
  Will gently shine ;—
Dawn which doth for the day prepare.

"I SHALL BE SATISFIED."

NOT here! not here! not where the sparkling
  waters
Fade into mocking sands as we draw near;
Where in the wilderness each footstep fal-
  ters;—
I shall be satisfied—but oh, not here!

Not here—where every dream of bliss deceives
  us,
Where the worn spirit never gains its goal;
Where, haunted ever by the thought that
  grieves us,
Across us floods of bitter memory roll.

There is a Land where every pulse is thrilling
  With rapture earth's sojourners may not
  know;
Where Heaven's repose the weary heart is
  stilling,
And peacefully life's time-toss'd currents
  flow.

Far out of sight, while yet the flesh infolds us,
  Lies the fair country where our hearts abide;
And of its bliss is naught more wondrous told
      us
  Than the few words, " I shall be satisfied ! "

Satisfied ! satisfied ! the spirit's yearning
  For sweet companionship with kindred
      minds,—
The silent love that here meets no returning,
  The inspiration which no language finds?

Shall they be satisfied ?—the soul's vague
      longings,
  The aching void which nothing earthly fills ?
Oh, what desires upon my soul are thronging,
  As I look upward to the heavenly hills !

Thither my weak and weary feet are tending—
  Saviour and Lord, with Thy frail child abide;
Guide me towards home, where, all my wan-
      derings ending,
  I then shall see *Thee*, and " be satisfied ! "

IS IT SO ?

Is it so, O Christ in Heaven, that the highest
　　suffer most ?—
That the strongest wander farthest and most
　　hopelessly are lost,
That the mark of rank in nature is capacity
　　for pain,
And the anguish of the singer makes the
　　sweetness of the strain ?

Is it so, O Christ in Heaven, that whichever
　　way we go,
Walls of darkness must surround us, things
　　we would, but cannot, know,
That the Infinite must bound us as a temple
　　veil unrent,
While the Finite ever wearies, so that none
　　attain content ?

Is it so, O Christ in Heaven, that the fullness
　　yet to come
Is so glorious and so perfect that to know
　　would strike us dumb,
That if only for a moment we could pierce be-
　　yond the sky,
With these poor dim eyes of mortals, we should
　　. just see God and die ?

SORROW.

SHOULD Sorrow lay her hand upon thy shoul-
    der,
  And walk with thee in silence on life's way,
While Joy, thy bright companion once, grown
    colder,
  Becomes to thee more distant day by day ;
Shrink not from the companionship of Sorrow,
  She is the messenger of God to thee ;
And thou wilt thank Him in His great To-
    morrow,—
  For what thou know'st not now, thou then
    shalt see ;—
She is God's Angel, clad in weeds of night,
With whom " we walk by faith, and not by
  sight."

GRAVES.

THE new-made grave lies bare and brown
  Beneath the spring's capricious sky,
The chilly raindrops on it beat,
  The breezes pass it coldly by ;

14

But day by day Time's fingers work
   Their noiseless miracles of grace ;
Soft grasses wrap it greenly round ;
   The daisy lifts its starry face ;
The wild rose sends a honeyed breath
   To woo the bee from neighboring wold ;
The violet holds its dainty cup
   To catch the morning's earliest gold ;
The zephyrs round it linger long
   To stir the grass and rob the flowers ;—
It seems a child of Nature's own,
   Conceived upon her happiest hours.

So in our hearts the new-made graves
   Rise, desolating all the scene,
Till Time's light touches wreathe them round
   With clinging memories evergreen,
And radiant hopes that blossom out
   In Grief's soft fall of tender dew,
Till life is rich with growing wealth
   Of peaceful trust and insight new.
We see with eyes that shine through tears
   God's wondrous plan in light unfold ;—
We now would nevermore exchange
   Those flower - grown mounds of fertile
   mould

For any face whose smile grew soft
  Against our own in life's young prime ;—
In Paradise hearts grow not cold,—
  Our loved are There—we wait God's time !

———

COUPLETS OF COMFORT.

I.*

DESPAIR not in the vale of woe,
Where many joys from suffering flow.

II.

Oft breathes Simoom, and close behind
A breath of God doth softly blow.

III.

Clouds threaten, but a ray of light,
And not of lightning, falls below.

IV.

Thy branches are not bare—and yet
What storms have shook them to and fro !

V.

To thee has time brought many joys,
If many it has bid to go ;

VI.

And seasoned has with bitterness
Thy cup, that flat it should not grow.

VII.

Trust in that veilèd hand, which leads
None by the path that he would go ;

VIII.

And always be for change prepared,
For the world's law is ebb and flow.

IX.

Stand fast in suffering, until He
Who called it, shall dismiss also ;

X.

And from the Lord all good expect,
Who many mercies strews below ;

XI.

Who in life's narrow garden-strip
Has bid delights unnumbered blow.

"LIKE AS A FATHER.'

LIKE as a father, when his children weary
  In the dim path he knows so straight and
    plain,
Pities their sorrows, knows how sad and
    dreary
  Life seems to them—yet leads them on
    again ;—

E'en so our Lord, in this our time of sorrow,
  When our hearts faint and all earth's wells
    seem dried,
Pities His children, and doth let us borrow
  Help from that Heaven where our hearts
    abide.

He knows our frames ; He knows we are but
    groping,
  As children in the darkness, for His hand ;
He leads us on,—not seeing, only hoping,—
  And waiting patiently for His command.

LIFE THROUGH DEATH.

A DEWDROP falling on the wild sea wave,
Exclaimed in fear,—" I perish in this grave ;"
But in a shell received, that drop of dew
Unto a pearl of marvelous beauty grew ;
And, happy now, the grace did magnify
Which thrust it forth—as it had feared, to
    die ;—
Until again, "I perish quite," it said,
Torn by rude diver from its ocean bed.
O unbelieving !—so it came to gleam
Chief jewel in a monarch's diadem.

———

THE TWO VOICES.

" All things are reconciled
In Thee, O Lord ! all fierce extremes that beat
Along Life's shore,
Have crept to kiss Thy feet ! "

' OVER the world the snow flakes are lying,
Cold as the lips that have done with sighing,
    Freezing the breath of the hours ;
Hiding the sod from the warm sun-glances,
Shutting the mold from the blithe rain-dances,
    Muffling the trees and the bowers ! '

'*Yet 'neath the coldness some warmth is abiding,*
Under the frost-belt the grain-roots are hiding,
  Under the snow, the flowers.'

'Over the earth glad verdure is springing,
Birds sweetest matins and vespers are singing,
  Rivers in harmony flow ;
Out in the fields the grain-gold is gleaming,
Over the meadows the sun-gold is streaming,
  Flowers unfold in the glow !'

'*Yet of the summer the life is abating,*
Back of the sunshine the storm-cloud is waiting,
  Back of the flowers, the snow.'

'Dark, in my life, the shadows are growing,
Into its gardens the thick cares are snowing,
  Wide opens sorrow's abyss ;
Smiling is changed into bitterest weeping,
Love o'er its graves mournful vigil is keeping,
  Never was darkness like this !

'*Yet in the shadow hope's soft wing is glowing,*
Out of the night-time the morning is growing,
  Out of life's sorrow, its bliss.'

' Down in my heart sweet blossoms are spring-
ing,
Ripplings of music and snatches of singing
Meet in its cheery refrain ;
Freshest of garlands Hope's fingers are weav-
ing,
Love to her promises listens believing, •
Life is all sunshine again ! '

' *Yet in the carol an undertone waileth,*
After the sunlight the black shadow traileth,
After life's gladness, its pain.'

' Teach me, O Father ! this truth to discover,
That in the snow-flakes which over us hover,
Skies all agloom or aflame,
Grief that depresses, or gladness that raises,
I of Thy love read the manifold phrases,
Love that is ever the same ! '

' *Trust in that love through the joy and the*
sorrow,
Changeless is He both to-day and to-morrow,
LOVE is forever His name.'

THE STRANDED SHIP.

2 Chron. xxxvi. 15, 16.

I SAW a vessel which the waves did spare
   Lie sadly stranded on a sandy beach,
      Beyond the tide's kind reach ;
Within its murmur of lamenting speech
      Long lay she there ;
      Until at length
A mighty sea arose in all its strength,
      And launched her lovingly.
      And thus, alas! our race
Lay stranded on the beach of human sin
      And misery,
Beyond all help, until God's glorious grace—
      A mighty tide,
      All crimson dyed—
      Swept grandly in
      And set us free.

THE COMMON OFFERING.

IT is not the deed that we do,
 Though the deed be never so fair,
But the love that the dear Lord looketh for,
 Hidden with holy care
 In the heart of the deed so fair.

The love is the priceless thing,
 The treasure our treasure must hold,
Or ever the Lord will take the gift,
 Or tell the worth of the gold
 (By the love that cannot be told).

Behold us, the rich and the poor,
 Dear Lord, in Thy service drawn near ;
One consecrateth a precious coin,
 One droppeth only a tear,—
 Look, Master, the love is here.

———

ALPHA AND OMEGA.

ALPHA and Omega :
Be Thou my First and Last,—
 The Source whence I descend,
 The Joy to which I tend,
When earth is past.

Open my waking eyes,
And fill them with Thy light;
  For Thee each plan begun,
  In Thee each duty done,
Close them at night.

Enfold me when asleep;
Let soft dews from above
  Refresh the long day's toil,
  Wash off the worldly soil,
And strengthen love.

Men speak of Four Last Things,—
Death, and the Judgment hall,
  Hell, and the Heaven so fair;
  But Thou, O Lord, art there,
Beyond them all.

There is no "last" with Thee,
But only our last sins,
  Last sorrows, and last tears,
  Last sicknesses, last fears,—
Then Joy begins;

Joy without bound or end,—
  Concentric circles bright,
  Spreading from round Thy throne,
  Flowing from Thee alone,
O Love! O Light!

Lay Thy right hand of power
In blessing on my brow ;
  Heaven's keys are in Thy Hand,
  Its portals open stand ;
I fear not now.

Lead Thou me gently in,
Thou who through death hast passed ;
  Then bring me to Thy throne,
  For Thee I seek alone,
My First and Last.

———

ELIM.

WHEN founts of Marah on our way
  Gush suddenly and strong,
How quick is Discontent to say,
  " O Lord, how long ? "

But when fair Elims bless our eyes
  With springing wells and palms,
Is Gratitude as swift to rise,
  And sing glad psalms ?

THE RACE.

LORD, Thou dost know
How weak my footsteps are, how slow
　　To run the race
　　Of Thy grace;—
Bound with the chain of dark, besetting sin,
　　While others move apace;
Yet I, through Thee, the victory shall win.
Although I be the last to enter in,
　　Thou still wilt wait,
And for my little strength wilt open keep Thy
　　gate.

———

THE HOLY NAME.

RINGING softly in mine ear,
　　Like a distant vesper bell,
With a silver sound and clear,
　　Is the name I love so well !

All the music upon earth,
　　Every tone of rarest fame,　　.
Hath its pure, harmonious birth
　　From the music of that name.

Notes of life's full octave ring
  In that chord—a mystic seven ;
And from that one key-note spring
  All the harmonies of heaven.

When it soundeth through the soul,
  Ah, how sweet, how clear and low !
Into one melodious whole
  All earth's jarring discords flow ;

Doubt and anguish melt away,
  And the spirit drifts along,
Toward the dawning of the day,
  On a silver tide of song.

Name of blessing—name of strength !
  Name of life—our joy and boast !
Oh, to sing Thy praise at length
  'Mid Thine own triumphant host !

Name of Jesus—name of love !
  Name at which I bend the knee !
Name all other names above—
  Oh, to love Thee boundlessly !

Lord my God ! On that dread day
  When Thy books unclosed shall be,
By Thine own dear name, I pray,
  May *my* name be known to Thee !

Grant that while I yet have time,
  Lest my soul be brought to shame,
All my steps may ever chime
  With the music of Thy name !

———

ADORATION.

I LOVE my God, but with no love of mine,
    For I have none to give ;
I love Thee, Lord, but all the love is Thine,
    For by Thy life I live.
I am as nothing, and rejoice to be
Emptied, and lost, and swallowed up in Thee.

Thou, Lord, alone, art all Thy children need,
    And there is none beside ;
From Thee the streams of blessedness pro-
  ceed,
    In Thee the blest abide,—
Fountain of life, and all-abounding grace,
Our source, our center, and our dwelling-
  place.

A TWILIGHT THOUGHT.

THE day is dead.   The stealing night
   With soft, dusk foldings blinds mine eyes ;
   Dear Christ, within my heart arise,
And cheer its dark with heavenly light !

The daylight hours I slow retrace
   To find some good thing said or done,
   Some battle-ground from evil won,
Where I may meet Thee face to face,—

And hear Thy sweet, commending word,—
   " Well done, thou servant good and true !"
   But ah ! mine eyes are wet with dew
Of disappointed tears, O Lord !

More battles I have lost than won,
   More ill than good unthinking wrought ;
   Naked I stand before my thought,
And scourge myself, and cry, " Undone !"

Undone, indeed, if Thou dost seek
   To find in me some smallest spot
   Where good doth reign, and sin is not !
My strongest powers are proved so weak—

My highest aims do fall so low !
  And all I think, or do, or say,
  Is soiled by touch of human clay,
Or dimmed with mist of human woe.

So, Lord, if Thou should'st be extreme
  To mark what is amiss in me,
  The pearly gates I ne'er shall see,
Nor tread upon the sunny gleam

Of golden streets, nor stand beside
  The sweet Life-river's crystal flow,
  Nor e'er the song of ransom know,
Nor look on Thee—the Crucified !

Lo ! at Thy cross I lay me down,
  And reckon o'er Thy groans and cries,
  Thy drops of blood, Thy agonies,
The thorns that wove Thy mocking crown,—

And list Thy cry of deep despair ;—
  And though my heart is like to break
  That thou should'st suffer so, I take
In every pang some comfort rare.

For surely, *surely*, not in vain
  Did'st Thou such anguish undergo,—
  Such dreary depth of soundless woe !
Such dread, surpassing weight of pain !

15

No human sin so black or deep,
  But Thou did'st full atonement make ;
  No soul can so with terror quake
But at Thy cross its fears may sleep.

So at its foot I lay me low,
  And tell Thy suff'rings o'er and o'er,
  And feel hope quicken more and more,—
And till Thou bless me, will not go !

———

THE SEA-BIRD.

In a plowed field I saw a sea-bird rest,
  Driven by the tempest inward from the sea ;
The gleaming plumage of its snow-white
    breast—
Fit only for the billow's kindred crest—
All sullied by the mold of the damp earth.
            Alas ! that we,
God's higher creatures, of a nobler birth,
  Should, sea-bird like, in cowardice forsake
The mighty ocean of God's higher will,
  When storms of persecution rise and break,
And when the waters are no longer still,
For the poor shelter of an inland hill,—
            Shrinking from toil,
Contented with the rest of this world's soil !

GOD'S ANVIL.

PAIN'S furnace-heat within me quivers,
  God's breath upon the flame doth blow ;
And all my heart in anguish shivers,
  And trembles at the fiery glow :
And yet I whisper, " As God will ! "
And in His hottest fire hold still.

He comes, and lays my heart, all heated,
  On the hard anvil, minded so
Into His own fair shape to beat it
  With His great hammer, blow on blow !
And yet I whisper, " As God will ! "
And at His heaviest blows hold still.

He takes my softened heart and beats it ;
  The sparks fly off at every blow ;
He turns it o'er and o'er, and heats it,
  And lets it cool, and makes it glow.
And yet I whisper, " As God will ! "
And in His mighty hand hold still.

Why should I murmur ? for the sorrow
  Thus only longer-lived would be :
Its end may come, and will, to-morrow,
  When God has done His work in me.
So I say, trusting, " As God will ! "
And trusting to the end, hold still.

He kindles for my profit purely
　　Affliction's glowing, fiery brand ;
And all His heaviest blows are surely
　　Inflicted by a Master-hand.
So I say, praying, " As God will ! "
And hope in Him, and suffer still !

———

THE MER DE GLACE.

Isaiah, li. 10, 11.

LORD, since Thy Christ hath walked death's
　　sea,
　　It lieth calmed,
Its tossing waves in solid ice embalmed,—
A footing firm, if cold, o'er which we pass :
　　And though this " Mer de Glace "
Hideth full many a deep and dark crevasse.
Yet o'er its desolation, calm and white,
The moon of faith sheds forth a tender light,
　　Which unto us doth show
His crimson footsteps on the frozen snow,—
Forming the track of immortality
　　Through death for us to Thee.

NOT LOST.

CONTENT thee ; in dear Paradise
　　There waits a day
Smiling for thee when shadows here
　　Have passed away.

And standing 'neath the joyous palms,
　　To thee 'twill seem
That all the years and tears wept out
　　Are one faint dream.

He gives us, and He gives us not,—
　　Our God can wait,—
And His best gifts He keeps for us,
　　Nor gives too late.

No smile is lost for evermore,
　　Lost is no love ;
They wander home to wait for us
　　In joy above.

———

"BUT BE YE GLAD, AND REJOICE."

Do we not pitch our songs too low,
　　O sweet my fellow-singers ?
Too oft alone life's paths we go
　　Like funeral-bell ringers.

Too much we sing of pain and loss,
  Of grief and desolation ;
Is there no sunshine from the cross ?
  No gladness in salvation ?

Too oft we strike the somber chord
  Of sin's depressing story ;
Too loud we chant, " Have mercy, Lord ! "
  Too faintly, "Give God glory ! "
If Grief must modulate the strain
  Into a mournful minor,
Strong Faith should quickly soar again
  In major chords diviner.

Our path is not so very rough,
  Our sky so very dreary ;
There's always ease and light enough
  To keep some corner cheery.
Why note so well each flying cloud,
  That casts a hand-broad shadow,
And overlook the beams that flood
  The whole wide-blooming meadow ?

" Till *now*," said Paul in olden days,
  " The whole creation groaneth ;
But he who walks in heavenly ways
  A weight of glory owneth."

Ah ! even yet our love for Christ
    Too often " lies a-bleeding,"—
How can we go to His sweet tryst
    Without a "joy exceeding"?

Oh, let us tune our harps again,
    And raise the pitch up higher,
And join on earth the gladsome strain
    That thrills the heavenly choir,—
Forget to sing of sin and fear,
    Of woe and consolation,
And let our voices ring out clear
    In songs of exultation !

We ask the watchmen on the hills,—
    "What cheer ? What sign of dawning ? "
Like music sweet the answer thrills,—
    " Night broods—but comes the morning."
Be that the word we pass along,—
    " Night broods (for rest, not sadness) ;
But morning comes ! Leap, heart ! wake song !
    We scarce can rest for gladness ! "

HYMN.

Rerum Deus tenax vigor.

O THOU true life of all that live !
Who dost, unmoved, all motion sway ;
Who dost the morn and evening give,
And through its changes guide the day :

Thy light upon our evening pour,—
So may our souls no sunset see ;
But death to us an open door
To an eternal morning be.

Father of mercies ! hear our cry
Hear us, O sole begotten Son !
Who, with the Holy Ghost most high,
Reignest while endless ages run.

INDEX OF FIRST LINES.

233